CHASING NORMALITY

With a Little Help from Family and Friends

A Memoir

By

Richard L. Wieler

With

Maureen O'Halloran Clark

Thanks!

Chasing Normality

© 2009 Richard L. Wieler

Written with Maureen O'Halloran Clark

Cover Photo by Katherine McHaney Coker

Cover Graphic Design by Katja Smith

Printed in the United States of America.

Publisher: RMKM6 Publishing L.L.C.
            1174 I Road
            West Point, Nebraska 68788

ISBN:978-0-9842773-0-8

Printed by Morris Publishing®
            Kearney, NE

To purchase additional copies contact
RMKM6 Publishing LLC or
visit www.chasingnormality.com

To Wild Dick Wieler

July 13, 1956

If I could do what I'd like to do,
It would really be a sight,
For who ever heard of riding the moon
To chase the stars at night.

I'd gallop in front of the Man in the Moon
And wade through the Milky Way,
And find my way home by the Northern Lights
Before the break of day.

But such silly things weren't meant to be,
So I just sit and sigh,
I take my ride in fantasy
Across the clear blue sky.

I discovered this poem only recently, nestled among a pile of clippings about me collected faithfully by Mom over the years. It is written on a plain sheet of paper with no marks or identification whatsoever. By the date, it was created during my stay at St. Joseph's Rehabilitation Center in Omaha. I have no memory of the author; most of my memories about that lowest period of my life have been repressed, thankfully. The poem is a whimsical allusion to a universe far removed from the grim reality of a polio ward. Such is the power of fantasy. The human spirit, fueled in part by dreams, is not shackled by the bounds of physical realities. I dedicate this book to dreamers everywhere, and to all those who labor to make dreams come true.

Dick Wieler
April, 2009

CONTENTS

Section One: Forever Changed

Chapter 1   Polio's Onslaught 9

Chapter 2   Farm Boy 15

Chapter 3   Polio's Aftermath 24

Section Two: Rehabilitation

Chapter 4   Union Station 37

Chapter 5   Introduction to Warm Springs 41

Chapter 6   Southern Living 47

Chapter 7   Superintendent Andersen 62

Section Three: Getting Into College

Chapter 8   Uncle LeRoy & Aunt Joanie to the Rescue... 69

Chapter 9   Adventure in South Dakota 77

Chapter 10 College Student without a College 87

Section Four: University of Missouri

Chapter 11   On My Own ……………………….….... 92

Chapter 12   Independence: The Challenges …………. 101

Chapter 13   Law School …………………………….. 112

Chapter 14   Adaptations …………………………….. 128

Chapter 15   The Bar Exam …………………………. 136

Section Five: Attorney for Missouri

Chapter 16   Transition ……………………………….141

Chapter 17   Ross Young …………………………….. 147

Chapter 18   Real Life ……………………………….. 161

Chapter 19   Relationships …………………….…....... 174

Chapter 20   Back to the Beginning ……………….… 187

Chapter 21   Another Point of View …………….….. 197

Epilogue …………………………………….….. 211

Acknowledgments ……………………………… 215

About Us ……………....……………………….. 217

CHASING NORMALITY

With a Little Help from Family and Friends

1

Polio's Onslaught

"Open your mouth, son," Dr. Anderson said. The examination was swift and he left the room hurriedly. I was told later that he issued an immediate command: "Isolate this boy, he has polio." That night, in violation of orders, I got out of bed to go to the bathroom. It was the last time that I would ever stand or get out of bed on my own. The next morning, I tried to sit up but my arm lacked the strength to lift a shoulder from the bed.

Things were deteriorating rapidly. As the paralysis spread, my breathing became labored and shallow. Life was ebbing away in that isolated hospital room. I was no longer aware of daylight or darkness; even the light seemed to be dimming. Death had come to call, not with a roar or a loud bang, but softly, quietly.

With two exceptions, I have no memory of the next few days. I remember being given the last rites of the Catholic Church, Extreme Unction. After that, I recall someone saying that I was to be placed in an apparatus of some type to assist with breathing. I remember thinking this seemed like a good idea; I felt like a tractor was sitting on my chest. Shortly thereafter, I lapsed into a coma.

A few words in praise of my parents are in order at this point. This is their story too, a story of love and devotion. In the space of one short week, our lives were changed forever. Death had indeed come to call for a member of the family. My sister Diane was admitted to the hospital three days after me, suffering from many of the same symptoms. She celebrated a very quiet twelfth birthday on September 9, 1955, and died swiftly the next day. Diane was killed by a brutal attack of bulbar polio, the type which attacks the brain directly.

The sudden and heartbreaking loss of a child had happened to another generation of my family. Both of my parents had witnessed the death of sisters under tragic circumstances. Mom's little sister, Darlene, died of a ruptured appendix at age three. Dad's little sister, Angela, fell on a jagged piece of farm equipment while playing with Dad and his brother. She died in my grandfather's arms as he was rushing her by train to a brain specialist in Omaha. Like Darlene, she too was only three years old. As my parents buried their only daughter, they kept constant vigil over me as I fought for my life. At the same time, they lived with the fear that the virus might strike yet more members of the family, including their youngest son, my five-year-old brother Michael.

It was the beginning of a long and often painful journey into the unknown. Before being stricken, I had enjoyed my annual summer routine on the farm. Among other things, I celebrated my 15th birthday in early August. With the school year looming,

My sister Diane

I participated in one of the last rites of summer; the annual county fair. I entered several items for exhibition that year, including the wooden picnic table I built in vocational agriculture shop. When it won a blue ribbon at the county fair, my teacher urged me to take it to the state fair at Lincoln, Nebraska. A group of us students accompanied him to Lincoln on September 2nd with the exhibits, and helped set them up in the exhibition hall. On my return, I felt an unusual sense of tiredness. I awoke the next day, Saturday, with a severe headache and a stiff neck. After struggling through the morning chores, I spent most of the afternoon walking about the family farm trying to shake it off. As usual, my border collie, Lassie, was my faithful companion. She realized quickly that this was to be no frolic; my mood was too dark. After several feeble attempts at play, she was content to walk by my side. That night, the symptoms worsened. The next morning, my parents decided to take me to the local hospital. Our young family physician diagnosed the problem as the flu but hospitalized me as a precaution. Sunday night passed uneventfully and the continued bed rest on Monday seemed to relieve the symptoms, although I still felt weak.

Dr. Anderson popped in some time on Monday, or perhaps Tuesday. Every small town in America has had its Dr. Anderson, the local legend who eschewed the big city to practice medicine in a rural community. He was everywhere, or so it seemed, birthing babies, tending to the sick, operating on somebody's uncle, or offering condolences to grieving families. Dr. Anderson's kind has buildings, memorials, and parks named after them in small towns everywhere because of the respect their patients felt for them. Anderson Memorial Field is West Point's tribute. "Doc's" patients knew his concern was genuine, his medical skills excellent, his commitment total, and his bedside manner impeccable. When called on for consultation, Dr. Anderson's long experience allowed him to make the swift and correct diagnosis. Without a doubt, he knew polio when he saw it.

The disease ran its frightful course while I was unconscious. Like Gulliver, I woke up a week later to a whole new world. With the exception of facial muscles, I was paralyzed. The apparatus I had been placed in was an iron lung; I was dependent upon it for breath. I was unaware of my sister's death or funeral, of my parents' agony, or of anything else. My only reality was the long cylindrical tube with a foam rubber collar that fit tightly around my neck.

As the fever receded, I became more conscious of my surroundings. Nothing seemed to exist below my neck. I could speak freely as long as I timed my response to the rhythm of the machine. No congestion had developed in my lungs so a tracheotomy had been unnecessary. Also, I had no difficulty swallowing, so various tubes were removed as the days passed, and I began to eat regular food. The bladder returned to normal function, so the catheter was removed.

However, I remained totally dependent on the iron lung for breathing. Anytime the lung was opened and the seal broken, I was unable to breathe on my own. An iron lung has a series of portholes along each side which can be opened when a caregiver needs to perform some function inside. Once an arm is thrust into a porthole, a foam rubber collar closes around it to maintain the pressure needed to pull the occupant's chest cavity up and down.

One of the round-the-clock nurses pressed into service on my behalf was rather old and somewhat forgetful. Whenever called upon to perform a function inside the cylinder, she invariably forgot to close the porthole afterwards. With the seal thus broken, I was unable to talk or breathe. Once she noticed the blue tinge on my cheeks, the search to rectify her mistake was undertaken, usually accompanied by the muttered exclamation,

"Oh, dear, oh dear." It seemed like she went to the wrong side of the lung every time. Once the open porthole was found and closed, I would get my much-needed breath. It felt too good to waste by complaining.

Two of my regular nurses were young sisters from the order of Franciscan Sisters of Christian Charity, Sister Alanna and Sister Mary Felice. The Franciscan Sisters have been part of the fabric of this community since 1885. Throughout the years, they have cared for the sick and the elderly in West Point, and educated our children. I was drawn quickly to these two by their compassion and loving care. Sister Mary Felice was a large and imposing figure in her white nun's habit, but she was quite cheerful and outgoing. I promptly dubbed her "Sister Tiny."

Life settled into a routine within the lung, including the periodic porthole episodes. Attempts were made daily to provide range-of-motion and other exercises, mindful always of the limitations imposed by the cylinder and the breathing problems which developed when the seal was broken. The maintenance man rigged a mirror above my face so that I could see people behind me who came to visit or work. Through that mirror, I watched the 1955 World Series between the Brooklyn Dodgers, and my then-team, the New York Yankees. Watching through a mirror meant that everything looked backwards. It seemed like runners were headed to third base instead of first on base hits. That was the year the Dodgers finally broke through the Yankee dynasty, winning the series behind Johnny Padres' pitching and the fantastic catch in left field (right in my mirror) by Sandy Amoros off the bat of Yogi Berra. But the World Series wasn't the only thing that seemed backwards. As I lay in the iron lung, I had plenty of time to reflect on my turned-around life.

2

Farm Boy

The summer of 1955 had begun with great promise. Classes at Guardian Angels High School, the Catholic school in West Point, Nebraska, were dismissed on Memorial Day. As was the custom, we marched to the local cemetery to pay our respects and were then dismissed after receiving our final report card of the year. I had finished my sophomore year and I knew what to expect on my report card. It would reflect continued academic progress and several negative references to my conduct.

It was of little consequence to me. Freed from the constraints of the schoolroom, summer was the time to continue my practical education in farming. At age fourteen, with two years of high school behind me, I could see the end in a mere two years. Then I could take my place as the latest generation of the family on the farm. The thought was exhilarating, much more than any report card.

Educational policies were not so standardized in those days. I was allowed to begin formal education at age four when my parents and the public school teacher in the one-room grade school a mile from our farm home agreed that I was ready for kindergarten. School was never difficult from an academic standpoint; I got high marks all through grade school. However, being at least a year younger than my classmates in high school, my immaturity was keeping me from being a well-rounded student. Deportment was graded as well as subject matter, and my lack of it was duly noted with Ds and Fs.

According to the Franciscan sisters who ran Guardian Angels High School, my mastery of the subject matter was greatly diminished by a sassy attitude in class and a stubborn unwillingness to take directions without argument. In their opinion, such attributes were unbecoming to a good Catholic youngster. Worse than that, one nun, new to the community, had the temerity to suggest that my educational goals were set much too low. Not being from rural Nebraska, she had no understanding of the love of farming which was bred into us from birth. Yet, she and the other nuns spared no effort to grill us in the fundamentals of our religion, math, science, English, history, and the basics of good citizenship.

I had no ambition other than farming. My favorite subject was the two years of vocational agricultural training at the local public high school. I wore my blue Future Farmers of America jacket proudly, ever mindful of our teacher's admonition: "Your hometown is printed on the back of that jacket, don't embarrass it." That was one order I tried to follow without backtalk.

Everybody on Dad's side of the family was or had been a farmer. My grandfather came to eastern Nebraska in the early 1900s to seek his fortune in agriculture. Through sheer hard work, good financial management, and the luck of having arrived at the right place at the right time, he was able to leave a farm to each of his three sons.

Dad left school after the eighth grade to farm with his father. This was not unusual in those days; many people in my father's generation never finished high school. In the opinion of many, farming was best taught at home. The added labor was essential and school was necessary only to teach reading, writing and arithmetic.

Mom's roots were deep in the soil as well. Her father had farmed with his brother for many years on land belonging to their parents. After the brother's untimely death forced an estate sale in the 1930s, he moved his family to Omaha. There he worked as a commission salesman for a firm selling livestock on the Omaha market. I never knew him; he died an untimely death a year before my birth.

My love of reading definitely came from Mom's side of the family. Many of them saw value in "book learning" and had used education to broaden their horizons and expand their vocational opportunities. I could always count on my young aunts for a never-ending supply of books—books like *Huck Finn, Tom Sawyer, Ivanhoe, and Black Beauty.* They were often read at night under the covers by aid of a flashlight.

Reading was just a hobby though. Dad was in charge of my practical education. With his guidance, I was learning, among other things, the art of fattening cattle. Nebraska is known for its beef production. Eastern Nebraska funnels fattened beef through its dry lots to the slaughter houses and then to the nation. This enterprise became very profitable after the Second World War, and especially during the early '50s. It was that time in America when small family farms could be operated profitably. Inflation was relatively low, interest rates were low, and the tax burden had not reached the levels it would reach in subsequent decades.

Dad pursued his occupation with great zeal. He and a business partner used borrowed money to buy feeder cattle from the ranchers in the West and South, and the grain necessary to feed them. After approximately 120 days of intensive dry lot feeding, the fattened animals were ready for slaughter, corn fed beef for America's tables.

West Point is ideally situated for this type of activity. It is located in the heart of the best corn growing country in Nebraska, and sits almost midway between Omaha and Sioux City, Iowa. At the time, those were two of the major markets for the sale and slaughter of fattened cattle. Today, these stockyards no longer exist; the packers have relocated to rural areas closer to the source of supply. Then as now, large trucks fanned out in every direction to bring young cattle from the grass ranges where they were born and raised to be fattened in confined pens or dry lots. Our feedlots were bulging in the summer of 1955, a hired man and I spent several hours each day feeding twelve hundred of Dad's cattle.

I also had cattle of my own to feed. I was nine years old when Dad took me to the bank to conduct cattle business for the first time. He thought it extremely important that I learn the management techniques behind the successful business of cattle feeding, and not just the daily chores required to care for the animals, and fatten them. "Anybody can man a shovel," Dad used to say; he wanted me to use my brains as well and nine was soon enough by his reckoning to see if I had any.

After discussion with "Banker Bill" (Dad's term, but one common to most in the town, I'm sure), I emptied my savings account, borrowed money, and purchased my first load of feeder cattle to be fattened. Of course, Dad was instrumental in all of these decisions, including co-signer of every note at the bank, but I had to man the shovel. Twice every day, those cattle had to be fed, a combination of alfalfa hay, corn and a protein and vitamin supplement. At first, the young cattle would get mostly hay, but this was gradually diminished and the corn and supplement increased as they matured and accepted the fattening corn diet. Once on "full feed," cattle can eat an astonishing amount of corn, or so it seemed to a young boy with his shovel. Summer and winter, before school and after, I trudged out to the lot to feed my cattle in addition to the other assigned chores.

As the years passed, the profits from this enterprise became evident. I accepted all the gains and the losses, and learned how to maintain and balance my own checking account, from which all expenses and taxes had to be paid. The profits, and more borrowed money, were used to finance more purchases. By the summer of 1955, I had 110 head of cattle on feed, as well as ownership of a tractor, a corn cultivator, a plow, and a mower.

Since I was doing so well financially, Dad thought it appropriate that I buy the family's second car as well. He got no argument from me. The car was a new red and white Plymouth and I thought I was big stuff when I drove it to school. School permits were available to anyone age fourteen who lived in the country. Passing the driving test for the permit had been a snap; farm boys learn how to handle machinery early. Machinery is essential to successful farming, even more so today.

Happy Days in 1955 with my sister Diane and little brother Mike.

I was one proud car owner.

In addition to cattle feeding, we were active in general farming operations on our quarter section of land, a hundred and sixty acres (small by modern standards). Approximately one hundred and thirty acres were devoted to crop production, a continually rotated combination of corn, oats and alfalfa. Other livestock occupied some of our time as well. Hogs have always been the most efficient way of turning corn into meat and we maintained a small herd of breeding sows, fattening their litters for market. For some reason, Dad also kept a herd of sheep, seventy or so ewes and several rams. Taking care of them was my responsibility, and my skills as a midwife during lambing season had been improving.

Also, my skills with a tractor had reached a level where I was becoming an integral part of crop production around the neighborhood. In the '50s, agricultural machinery was not as sophisticated as it is today. Much of the work was labor intensive, and farmers often banded together to harvest crops. We worked with others where necessary to get our crops in, care for them, and harvest them at maturity. Community was a big part of farming. During summer, there was corn to be cultivated, oats to be harvested, and a seemingly endless round of hay to be worked.

In good economic times, life on the farm is a grand adventure for a kid. There was always work to be done and I was expected to do my share of it, but it never seemed burdensome. One year I asked Dad if I could take my birthday off. He just laughed. "Son, your birthday means nothing to those cattle out there and they come first." Sundays, holidays and birthdays were observed or celebrated before chores, between chores, or after chores. Dad's unwritten and mostly unspoken philosophy of farming, and life, was very simple: whatever the problem, work was the solution. If something went badly, you worked harder to overcome it; if something went well, you worked harder to capitalize on it. Even so, it was not all work; there was plenty of time to indulge in childhood fantasies. I did my share of playing—romping about the yard with my dog, riding horses, or pestering my younger sister and little brother.

A growing sense of maturity and independence allowed me to defy Dad's wishes in one area that summer. Much to his disgust, but with Mom's quiet support, I tried out for summer

Good times on the farm with Mike, Diane and our horses.

baseball and won a starting position with a "big midget" team in town. West Point has always had a love affair with baseball. There are still organized leagues for every age group, including an adult town team. On several occasions, I had to rush from the hay field, jump into my baseball uniform, and head for town. I was a pitcher on the team and judging from my record of no wins that summer, not a very good one. However, the coach kept giving me the opportunity to start because I was left-handed, a rarity in a small town. I could throw hard and I was "coachable" (in his opinion, an opinion obviously not shared by those in charge of my academic progress). Once I learned how to control my pitches, the sky was the limit, or so I thought. When time permitted, I spent hours throwing baseballs at a tire hanging on an old shed behind the grove. I nurtured dreams of making the American Legion team the next year.

With all that activity, the summer of 1955 seemed to be a dream come true. I was so busy living it that I never noticed the hot and dry weather, or the fact that cattle prices had leveled off and were starting to drop slowly. To me the next year would produce even bigger and better dreams. One catastrophic week in early September smashed those dreams forever. I was trapped in an iron cylinder wondering if I would ever breathe or walk on my own again. It was the beginning of a long journey, a journey that would test my character in ways unimaginable.

One thought never occurred to me. It wasn't until years later that I learned how close we were to being saved from the scourge of polio. Doctor Jonas Salk had tested his vaccine and proved that it would work by 1954. However, a mishap at one of the labs producing it meant that the vaccine was not available for mass distribution for the summer polio season in 1955. Dad made inquiries about it in the spring and was told it would be available in the fall, at the earliest. Sure enough, the vaccine arrived in the West Point area in late September. In life, timing is everything.

3

Polio's Aftermath

Polio is a virus that strikes at the base of the brain and the spinal column. The virus is very selective, choosing to attack the gray fatty substance in the spine known as the myelin. Therefore, unlike trauma induced spinal injuries, complete blockage between the brain and the body does not occur. All of the sensory receptors are left intact. The result is that the victim can still feel pain or discomfort. The inflammation simply disrupts the motor communication nerves between the brain and the muscles of the body. Paralysis results when the brain's orders are no longer communicated to the muscles.

Once the initial assault runs its course, the method of treatment is very simple. Keep the muscles alive and the body joints supple as long as possible by applying hot packs and by stretching the patient's limbs and moving them in range-of-motion exercises. Then it's a matter of waiting for the body to regenerate nerve endings to re-establish the communication path between the brain and the muscles. If the nerves do not regenerate within six months to a year, the muscles atrophy beyond use, although some polio victims have claimed limited return years later.

Five weeks had passed; the disease had run its course through my body. It was time to take the next step. The local hospital was not equipped to handle a long-term rehabilitation program so arrangements were made to transfer me to a hospital in Omaha, St. Joseph's Rehabilitation Center.

Since I was still unable to breathe on my own for more than a limited time without the lung, special preparations were made for the move. A truck and a special trailer with the capacity to carry an iron lung and the batteries necessary to power it during transit were brought to West Point. With one of the nursing sisters operating the manual pump at the rear of the iron lung, I was disconnected from the hospital's power supply and wheeled down the halls to the waiting truck. Once aboard and connected to the trailer's batteries, we set sail for the unknown.

Everything went smoothly for the first thirty miles until one of the batteries malfunctioned and the lung stopped working. Sister Tiny, who had gone along for the ride, was suddenly put to work again operating the manual pump. She stayed at her post for twenty minutes or so until the driver found a filling station. A power cord was run from the filling station outlet to the lung until the battery problem was resolved. The rest of the trip was uneventful, not that anybody noticed after such a scare. The real fright for me was about to begin. I was far from familiar surroundings, and very much alone.

The medical staff at St. Joseph's quickly determined that my rehabilitation program would be better managed outside of the iron lung. Tests revealed some return of diaphragm function, the principal muscle used for breathing. I could breathe on my own for short periods. Once outside, I could be subjected to a more complete range of physical therapy and breathing exercises. Skin care could be more readily managed as well. I had developed several decubitus ulcers (bed sores) from lying in one position in the lung: one at the base of the neck where the foam rubber collar fit so tightly, and one at the base of the spine. This pressure could be relieved and the sores better treated by frequent turning outside the lung.

However, in five short weeks the iron lung had become the center of my universe. I was alive, and even secure in my steel cocoon. I was terrified at the prospect of life outside that lung. No matter how limited, it seems we all try to live within the edge of our known world. What lies within is familiar and comforting, what lies without is dangerous and unknown. But, the staff was insistent, and they were in control. The iron lung was broken apart and I was raised to a sitting position. For the first time since the initial onslaught of the disease, I was subjected to pain, intense pain. Muscles and joints that had not been moved for five weeks were forced into motion. The combination of dizziness, pain, and terror reduced me to babbling incoherence. "No, No, No," was all I could say. For the first time, I saw the effects of paralysis. I saw my arms dangling at my side, useless; I saw my legs dangling over the side of the lung bed, useless. Without the firm grip of staffers, I would have pitched forward into a crumpled heap on the floor.

The first order of business, as always, was breathing. I was still very much ventilator-dependent and further mechanical assistance was imperative. After being placed on a bed, I was fitted with a chest cuirass, or chest ventilator. This is a small hard-shelled device, much like a turtle shell. When fitted properly over the chest, negative pressure is supplied in regular intervals through a vacuum hose attached to a power source. The suction pulls the diaphragm upward and then releases it to stimulate breathing. I soon realized that it served its purpose quite well and my terror at leaving the iron lung subsided.

My known world had just been expanded. The iron lung became less the savior and more the necessary monster whose services were no longer required. For the first time in five long weeks, I could be moved freely about a bed. Now, much less effort was required to deal with every ache and pain, every wrinkle in the sheet under me, or any foreign object lodged against my skin. Also, I could see my new world without the limiting frame and distortion of a mirror.

I began to take note of my new neighbors. They were a mixed lot to say the least. There were six of us in the ward, an acute care ward. We were separated only by curtains and united by a common terror—the baffling condition of paralysis. Polio played no favorites; we ran the gambit from frightened and bewildered teenagers to several older professionals, including two lawyers. We had another thing in common—pain! The term "range-of-motion" assumed a whole new meaning as I was subjected to it twice a day, and watched my ward mates subjected to the same.

The procedure was simple enough: first, blazing hot packs (rags heated in some steam device) were placed on the arms and legs. Then, a therapist would stretch the muscles, ligaments, and joints, trying always to approach the normal range for each joint.

Inactivity always stiffens joints, and muscles lose their elasticity, so a great deal of force was applied to maintain range. At times, the pain was so intense that tears were involuntary. Therapy was agonizing. On those occasions when I put aside my own misery long enough to look around, it seemed like the two lawyers coped the best. Perhaps, they were so schooled in mental activities that they were able to concentrate on intellectual pursuits in spite of physical punishment. Perhaps they were just older.

This went on day after day. As the months went by, I began to realize that the paralysis was not going to go away. Certain muscles responded, but none strong enough to overcome gravity. I could wiggle my toes and push down with my feet. I could move my head from side to side, but not lift it off the bed. I could not raise a leg or an arm, or roll over in any fashion. I was dependant, totally dependant, on the care of others. Some was delivered with skill and compassion, most with indifference. It appeared that the general sense of hopelessness in the ward had sapped the morale of the staff as well as the patients.

The most hopeful development in the early months at St. Joseph's was a slowly strengthening diaphragm. I could now breathe for longer periods of time without mechanical ventilation. Within six months, I was switched from the chest shell to an even more benign form of assisted breathing, the rocking bed. A rocking bed is a bed mounted on a fulcrum, a motorized seesaw. The principle behind its usefulness is simple: as the head goes up and the toes go down, gravity pulls downward on the diaphragm to assist inhalation; as the toes go up and the head goes down, pressure against the diaphragm assists in exhalation. The cycle was repeated fourteen to eighteen times a minute. It must have been a sight to walk into that ward and see three or four of these rocking beds in action. Our lives were adrift on these mechanical seas, stopping only for therapy, linen changes and bathing.

The nurses in the ward were adept at feeding us without stopping the bed. It was a matter of moving the spoon or drink in synchronization with the bed's rocking motion. With a little practice, it could be done without mishap. However, more serious incidents were possible. I recall two. Once, a nurse inadvertently shoved a stool under the edge of a bed while it was in motion, causing it to tip over. The occupant, my "next door neighbor," had been rocking away in drugged serenity following minor surgery. Suddenly, he was pitched to the floor, bedding, I.V. bottles and all. No damage done, the bed was righted, he was retrieved, and the rocking continued. On another occasion, a rather stout nurse, heavily corseted, bent over to retrieve some soiled linen at the foot of a rocking bed. The footboard of the bed wedged between her bottom and the corset. The motor was powerful enough to catch her and hold her, writhing in embarrassment. Again, no damage done; just much needed comic relief for those in attendance.

Another bodily function returned to normality in sudden fashion. While getting a bed bath one morning, the action of the warm washcloth against my skin created a sudden and intense arousal. Every farm kid understands the basic nature of sexuality, having grown up around breeding animals. At my age, that knowledge had been expanded through locker room banter. My silent wonder turned into sudden humiliation when the hospital nun giving the bath whacked the offending organ swiftly with a pencil. No words were spoken, none were needed. Our common religious bond stressed that certain bodily function was reserved for the marriage bed. But I pondered this often in the lonely hours of the night. Marriage? Children? "Fool," was the silent rejoinder. Your body is mocking you with a normal sex drive; who is going to love a helpless, deformed cripple?

The psychological stress was beginning to take its toll. I realized I would never walk again, sometimes I wondered if I would ever leave St. Joseph's Hospital. Mom and Dad visited when they could but West Point was a long way away and there was a farm to run. Stomach pains and cramps were becoming everyday occurrences. At times, it seemed that everything I ate caused great distress. Friends of my parents who lived in the Omaha area cooked a wonderful Thanksgiving dinner for us, but I promptly threw mine up. I was wasting away, a literal collection of skin and bones. At the lowest point, my weight slipped below a hundred pounds.

A series of tests confirmed the suspicions—I had developed a peptic ulcer. With medication and diet, it was brought under control, somewhat. Good news was still in short supply though. I could now breathe on my own for days at a time, with mechanical assistance at night. But I could not sit upright and my time in a wheelchair was limited by lack of endurance. In spite of these limitations, one spring day I was told that I could be furloughed for the weekend. Home! Even though it was just a weekend, never did anything sound so exciting.

On the appointed day, Mom and Dad showed up for my brief outing. Cars in those days did not have head rests, so we

**During an early visit, I am unable to sit to visit with
Dad, Mom and Mike at St. Joe's.**

placed a board behind my back and head to keep my head upright. As skinny as I was, Dad had no trouble getting me into the front seat. We drove through the countryside, back to West Point, and back to my past.

Things had changed in my absence. The livestock market had crashed in the fall of 1955, and the family farm was on hard times. However, my spirits soared as we traveled down that long, familiar driveway.

First order of business was to see my dog. After Dad put me in the wheelchair, I called out to her. Hearing me, Lassie rushed forward to leap into my arms. There were no arms, only a familiar voice in a strange contraption which skittered away from her leap. That was the end of our reunion. Lassie wanted no part of the new reality, she yelped and took off. From that day forward, she would never get within twenty feet of the wheelchair.

The rest of the weekend was equally somber. The uneven ground around the place was ill-suited to a wheelchair. The three steps in front of our house that I used to leap in a single bound had become an architectural barrier. I was carried in and placed on the bed that I had vacated on my own in the distant past. Even so, it was still better than the daily torture of life in the ward. I was home, temporarily to be sure, but home.

The drive back to Omaha was even more somber but it was obvious that life at home would be a burden as well. Further rehabilitation was necessary. So, it was back to St. Joseph's and the daily range-of-motion exercises, and the continuing struggle to improve my breathing. Breathing treatments were designed both to expand lung capacity and strengthen breathing muscles. A positive pressure machine was used to expand the lungs. It looked like a vacuum cleaner and it blew air into the lungs under high pressure. At least my role here was passive. Other devices, blow bottles, were used to strengthen breathing muscles. I blew endless gallons of water from one blow bottle to another in an attempt to strengthen lung muscles.

Gradually, the diaphragm was strengthened enough to provide adequate ventilation for normal breathing without mechanical assistance. However, the subordinate breathing muscles around the rib cage were gone. Without these normal muscle groupings, the ribs had lost flexibility and the lungs were constricted. At best, my vital capacity was 1200 cubic centimeters, about eighteen to twenty percent of normal. I lacked the explosive cough necessary to expel secretions from the lungs. In all those months, I was fortunate indeed to have never developed pneumonia, or even a common cold.

The danger from respiratory infections was well-known on the ward. We all witnessed the daily struggle of one of our members. Jack had been a teacher in his former life, and the father of three young children. Although he was making progress on other fronts, recurring respiratory infections never allowed the physicians to close the tracheotomy that had been performed during the initial onset of polio. The poor chap was constantly being suctioned through the hole in his neck. Finally, after months of struggle, the infections were brought under control and his rehabilitation program completed. Jack was released from St. Joseph's in 1956. We heard that he died a week after returning home, choking to death on something lodged in his throat.

As the summer of 1956 wore down, I was rapidly approaching stalemate in my struggle with polio. Attempts at occupational rehabilitation were very limited because of lack of stamina and the pervasive paralysis. Without muscles, the back was developing a slight "C" curve which was being aggravated by sitting up and my continuing growth. Skeletal deformities, if allowed to develop dramatically, would interfere with the diaphragm. So I was fitted with a steel and leather corset running from the hips to the armpits in an attempt to provide some stability. Thus corseted, I could sit in a wheelchair for longer periods of time. However, the seat had to be well-padded because mine was not. Also, the neck muscles were exceedingly weak, especially those on the front, so an extended back on the wheelchair was necessary.

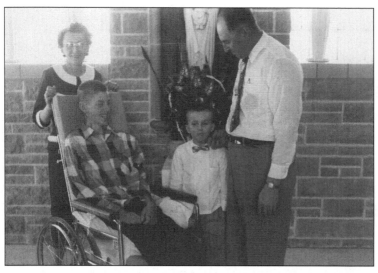

Wearing a corset, I could sit to visit my family at St. Joe's.

Since my arms lacked utility, I was introduced to the mouthstick. It is a simple invention to be sure, and one whose name suggests its function. The mouthstick, St. Joseph style, was a wooden dowel with a rubber tip on one end and a piece of rubber tubing on the other. Gripped by the teeth, it could be used to dial a telephone, turn the pages of a book, or any other use to which a stick held by the mouth might prove useful. Its best use for me turned out to be reading in bed. Using a specially designed reading stand, I read as much as possible. Reading material was always available from the two lawyers who seemed to have an inexhaustible supply of current events magazines.

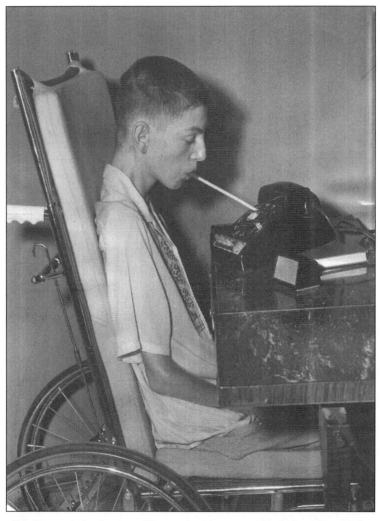

Dialing a telephone with a primitive mouthstick at St. Joe's

Mom and Dad were becoming increasingly frustrated by the slow pace of rehabilitation. On their visits to Omaha, they saw little or no progress being made. The proceeds from our health insurance policy were almost gone and our personal fortunes had diminished. Maintenance was all they witnessed, maintenance which could be done as well at home. Furthermore, for some reason they were convinced that more could be done, but not at St. Joseph's.

In the exit conference, my attending physician told them that I would be an invalid for the rest of my life, totally dependent on their care. He suggested that I might sell Christmas cards for a living and that their burden would be lessened greatly by my shortened life span. I am told this prognosis was angrily rejected. Mom and Dad simply refused to accept the doctor's view of a life with so little meaning for a sixteen-year-old son who had shown such promise before polio. And so, in September of 1956, I was released from St. Joseph's Hospital to the custody of my parents. The enormity of the task ahead of us was too difficult to imagine, but it was good to be out of the hospital. My journey through hell was over; it was time for a new beginning. But how?

4

Union Station

Even though the long and dreary year at St. Joseph's Rehabilitation Hospital had produced nothing beyond weaning me from the iron lung and other forms of mechanical breathing assistance, Mom and Dad still believed that something could be done to help me walk again and to regain the use of my arms and hands. They had heard about the Franklin Roosevelt Rehabilitation Center in Warm Springs, Georgia, which specialized in polio rehabilitation. They were Roosevelt Democrats, part of the coalition who admired Franklin Roosevelt for his leadership during the Great Depression and World War II. A decade after his death, details of Roosevelt's personal struggle with polio were becoming better known. If any place could help me, Warm Springs would be the place.

They applied for admission and to obtain funding they applied to the March of Dimes. Both applications were accepted and I was authorized to be admitted just before Christmas in 1956.

Although my parents had high hopes, I did not. The long year of separation and the transition from healthy active farm boy to helpless invalid had taken its toll. I was happy to be home, safely hidden from the daily grind of life in a city hospital and away from the outside world. At that point, I would have gladly accepted a life of seclusion, totally dependent on my parents for everything. There was no future for me.

I spent my days in front of the television. The brightest spot was watching Don Larson pitch a perfect game against the Dodgers in game six of the World Series. As a Yankee fan, I cheered every pitch as Dodger after Dodger failed to reach first base. Mom abandoned her disinterest in time to see a jubilant Yogi Berra leaping into Larson's arms after the final pitch.

"Oh, that poor man," she said. "After all that hard work he has to carry that fat guy off the field." Sorry, Yogi; Mom never did understand the finer points of baseball.

I dreaded the ordeal that lay ahead. Once again, I was to be separated from my family, and for what purpose? My experience with rehabilitation to that point had involved hours of hot packs followed by painful stretching exercises that kept the joints mobile but little else. What good would more of that do? However, the folks were committed. We drove to Chicago and stayed with some of Dad's relatives. They drove us to Union Station where we were to board the train to Atlanta, Georgia. Someone from Warm Springs would meet us there for the final seventy mile leg to our destination.

The noise and the commotion in Union Station were overwhelming. I had never been in a building so vast, or surrounded by so many people. The waiting room was huge, a tribute to the glory days of railroading. Appropriately it was called the Great Hall. Massive stone columns extended some 100 feet to a cathedral-high ceiling; the ceiling was an entire grid of skylights. I remember it because I had a clear view from my wheelchair reclined at a 45 degree angle. That was as far as I could sit up without support. My skinny rear couldn't tolerate the pressure of sitting upright for any length of time. I could see the cold polished pink-marble walls and I guessed the floor was more of the same. It radiated that coldness and the sound of my parents' footsteps along with the steps of thousands of other travelers hurrying to or from the trains.

Before paralysis, this would have been a grand adventure. But lying in a reclining wheelchair, I was mortified at being out in public, terrified at being among crowds. I did NOT want to be seen. There is some level of self-loathing at being paralyzed. I was shocked by my condition, even a full year after the onset. I think everyone who becomes paralyzed goes through that period initially. The loss of good health is a blow to one's self-esteem. I was so painfully aware that I was an object of pity and I did not care to be. In my peripheral vision I could see the mass of humanity; it seemed to me that everyone was staring down at me. I could see children pointing at me and tugging on their parents' legs. All I wanted to do was to run away, to hide from all the staring faces.

Now, 50 years later, I realize that the travelers were more intent on their own destinations and in their own worlds. I was not making a lasting impression on anybody; they probably were giving me a fleeting glance at best. But at the time, those glances were like a stab to the gut. I had developed a peptic ulcer during my year at St. Joe's and under stress I had the tendency to start puking. Thankfully, that didn't start until much later on the train.

The terror of being wheeled helplessly around the station was made even worse when we got to the boarding platform. Of course the train wasn't accessible. Dad and a porter picked me up and carried me up the steps, but they couldn't bend me enough to get around the corner. Dad was strong as a bull in those days and he quickly came up with a solution. He told the porter to hang on while he turned me on my side. Then they were able to bend me around the corner and safely deposit me on the bunk in one of the sleeping cars. When we arrived at Atlanta, we had to repeat the same process. I should have been a little lighter after spending the night throwing up. Mom had to hold my head up so I wouldn't aspirate. The expense of a sleeping car was mostly wasted; neither of us got much sleep.

It was a far cry from the self-sufficiency I had enjoyed a mere year and a half earlier when I could hop on my horse and go for a ride, or hop in my own car and go where I wanted within the limits set out by the law and Dad. I usually found a way to stretch those limits; I had been self-confident and my driving reflected it. Those days so long ago are pleasant memories now; on that train to Georgia, they were anything but. This was not the lowest moment of my experiences with polio but it certainly introduced me to the trials of public transportation for people with disabilities.

5

Warm Springs

It was a relief to arrive in Atlanta after a harrowing night on the train. A guy in a station wagon from the Foundation was there to pick us up and take us to Warm Springs, a tiny hamlet 70 miles south and west of Atlanta. He played raucous, southern music the entire 70 miles, too loud for conversation.

Propped up in the back seat next to Mom, I was driven through poor, rural country. Looking out the window, we saw a few cotton fields and some other signs of cultivation on land with red-hued soil. Here and there, battered tar paper shacks littered the landscape. People were living in those shacks. We saw chickens scrambling from beneath several of them as we drove past. Maybe it doesn't take much of a house to survive in a warm climate; at least that was our best guess. It was December but the temperature was much milder than it had been back in Chicago. Our road was a smooth two-lane paved highway but at random intervals little red dirt roads wandered into the countryside.

We couldn't imagine a world-class polio institution in the midst of this poor rural setting. I didn't know what to expect, but I was more than ready for relief from our driver's music. We were surprised by what we found at the end of the trail, a serene haven surrounded by pine forest at the edge of a small village of maybe 300 or 400 people. The town of Warm Springs itself was barely more than a crossroads.

The entrance was not spectacular, simply a gravel drive with a stone fence and stone pillars on either side of the turnoff. The drive wandered through the pines in a leisurely manner as we approached the grounds. We were amazed by our first view of the complex. The grounds were well-manicured and there were at least a dozen columned and white stately buildings. In addition, there was a cluster of large white houses to one side as well as a number of humbler but tidy cottages scattered about. We discovered later that many of the support staff lived in those cottages and houses. The Foundation was a small village unto itself. The main area consisted of a series of interconnected buildings surrounding a quadrangle. It looked more like a college campus than a hospital.

Our driver dropped us off at an entry point with two large white pillars guarding the door. Once our luggage was secured and I was safely in my wheelchair, Dad and I headed for the nearest restroom. Bursting in, we seemed to frighten the wits out of the two black men in there. We said "hello" to them, but they only nodded back and gave us the oddest look. We found that strange but finished our business and left. Only then did we notice the sign outside the door that read "Colored Only."

"What the hell is that all about," Dad said; "can you believe they have a bathroom for colored only?" It was 1956 and we were in the deep South; it was our first encounter with segregation. There was some protocol at work here that we were ignorant of; we wondered what the local whites would have said had they seen us exiting that bathroom.

This was my first exposure to something I had never seen in Cuming County, Nebraska. There were no blacks in the community where I grew up; I had never met a person of color face to face before being hospitalized in Omaha. Likewise, my dad was unsophisticated in the matter of race relations. Because the words tumbling from his mouth sometimes concealed the truth in his heart, I wasn't sure of his position on race. Still, I had never known him to refuse to extend his hand to a stranger, regardless of color.

Several decades later, I heard him state his beliefs quite simply. On that occasion, a sizable crew was preparing the street in front of my parents' retirement home for paving. It had been a gravel road before Dad led a petition drive to get it paved. Several people had gathered on the front deck to watch the proceedings. Noting the racial mix of the crew, one person said it was not quite right to see a black man running the large grader while whites were working with shovels and carpenter tools to prepare the area for the concrete. Dad said; "Baloney, he's in that cab because he knows what he's doing; look at the way he's handling that grader. I don't care if he's white, black, or green; anyone who works for a living is okay with me."

Mom spent some time as a working girl in Omaha before marriage and therefore had direct experience with other races. She thought people should be treated as individuals and I was taught to treat everyone with courtesy and respect, unless and until they gave me reason to do otherwise.

However, crusading for civil rights was the farthest thing from my mind. I didn't know what to expect in this whitewashed collection of buildings. Would this be another St. Joseph's Rehabilitation Center with me stuck in a ward with six other helpless individuals and subjected to endless rounds of painful physical therapy? I had been bracing myself to endure just that. How could it be anything different?

That's when I got my first glimpse of the Warm Springs "magic." Mankind has always found hot springs relaxing and healthful. Franklin Roosevelt had come here because of the opportunity to exercise in the warm waters bubbling from the ground and captured in a swimming pool. This area had once been a lively resort but it had fallen into decline when Roosevelt discovered it in the 1920s. Once word spread about his experience with the benefit of the warm waters, hordes of disabled people descended on the place. Roosevelt decided to buy the entire resort and turn it into an institution dedicated to the treatment of the after-effects of polio. By 1956, eleven years after his death, the Georgia Warm Springs Foundation (as it was called then) was the crown jewel in the fight against polio. Dr. Salk's vaccine had stopped the scourge of new cases but this place was humming with patients from earlier epidemics seeking treatment. With funding from the March of Dimes and its close association with the Roosevelt name, Warm Springs was staffed with experts in the field of rehabilitation. Many had come from other states and countries to study, learn, and train in the latest innovations for treatment. It was not a hospital for the acutely ill at all; it was an institution dedicated to restoring functional capabilities for those paralyzed by polio.

During our guided tour of the facilities, I discovered there weren't any wards in the place. There were single quarters for those who could care for themselves and a wing for people who needed more help. I was assigned a room in that wing, called the East Wing. All the rooms had huge windows that reflected the sunlight off the white exteriors. I was to have a single roommate. I noticed other rooms in the wing contained girls; segregation did not apply to the opposite sex. It did apply to black polio victims. Although few in number, they were confined to a basement wing.

One of the windows in my new room looked out into the inner quadrangle. Surrounded by the buildings, it must have been several acres in size, dotted here and there by large southern pines. Each building around the quadrangle had a distinct use. There was a surgical wing, the pool room, a large building dedicated to physical and occupational therapy on one level and a theater on the other, and a separate dining hall. Smaller buildings around the perimeter contained the brace shop, the schoolhouse, and the chapel. All of the buildings were connected in some way by a combination of elevators and long, wide hallways, as well as a series of covered walkways. People in wheelchairs or lying on carts were being pushed to and from the buildings by young men in white shirts and pants. It was a Warm Springs tradition—the young men were called "push-boys." They were responsible for getting patients to their various appointments, sometimes two or more at a time with a little help from the patients.

Another tradition was the dining hall. After we got situated, we were invited there for dinner. It was a gathering place for patients and staff alike, a large room with a huge chandelier and floor-to-ceiling windows on two sides. The dining hall served three meals a day but dinner was a special event. With separate tables covered by white tablecloths and set with fine dishes, good silverware and cloth napkins, it had the feel of a fancy restaurant. The head waiter, a black man nattily dressed in a tuxedo, stood guard at the door. He escorted us to our table and seated us properly. The irony of the situation was not lost on us. The head waiter and most of the kitchen staff were black and yet they weren't allowed to eat there. I decided to study this segregation in greater depth as time permitted. Was it simply custom or something far more sinister?

After dinner, I was told that only patients who could feed themselves were allowed to eat in the dinning hall. Others were fed in their room. I bid a silent goodbye to the dining hall. Since polio, my eating style could best be described as "baby robin." That is, I opened my mouth whenever food came near. Looking down on my helpless arms and hands as I lay in a reclined position, I was sure that would never change.

The introductory tour completed, it was time to say goodbye to Mom and Dad. That was very hard. I was still a young lad of sixteen, Christmas was coming, and Georgia was a long way from home. There would be no visits this time. I think the administrators at Warm Springs wanted a quick parting because they were stressing independence; clinging too tightly to family was detrimental to that goal. Before I could blink they were gone, back to Nebraska to deal with some grave financial problems. I wasn't told about it but a major restructuring was in the works. They needed to get ready for a big farm sale. Although the land was to remain in our hands, most of the machinery, including mine, would be sold to pay outstanding debts. While I was rehabbing in Warm Springs, Dad and Mom were starting over as well.

6

Southern Living

What happens now? This thought kept rolling through my head as I spent a sleepless first night in my new quarters. My roommate seemed affable enough but he wasn't much of a conversationalist. He was almost finished with his rehabilitation program and would soon be gone. I had no clue what lay ahead for me. My parents had returned to their world and I felt very lost and alone in mine.

Morning's first light swept away the fears as I was greeted with a cheery "hello" and breakfast. That was the only word I understood from this friendly black woman. I had been told about Southern accents; I didn't know it was a foreign tongue. It took a month to understand what I was being told without asking for a repeat. This put me on good terms with the black aides; they took great delight in my ignorance of the English language.

After breakfast, it was bath time; no bed baths here. The aides whisked me away on a cart to the tub room where I was lowered into a big high bathtub and scrubbed clean. I quickly learned that few things would take place in my room at Warm Springs. We weren't allowed to lie in bed under a hospital gown unless we were sick. The rehabilitation specialists didn't come to us; we went to them. The push-boys wheeled us around to our various assignments. At St. Joe's, I rarely left the one-room ward for any reason. There was nowhere to go and I was very ill during my initial recovery period.

Things were different for the patients at Warm Springs. It was an ideal setting for polios because we were healthy for the most part, other than the paralysis. This was my first time to interact with other polio people who were active. There were people scooting up and down the halls or outside in wheelchairs. Others were being pushed around in chairs or carts by the push-boys. There was romance going on in some of those halls. I was told that one of the patients had married one of the push-boys.

The first order of business for me was a complete medical evaluation. I was relieved that most of the staff assigned to that task were transplanted Northerners. Everybody spoke English. My physical therapist was a young woman from Canada, Berle Hambidge. She did a complete muscle and range-of-motion evaluation for the medical staff. She tested and dutifully recorded the massive muscle loss from the disease. More importantly, she noted the location and the strength level of the muscles that remained. Weak as they were, these muscles were to become the key to my future. Years later, I obtained a copy of the staff notes from my chart. The notes said, "There is nothing more we can do medically, surgically to improve the condition, but we can go with a functional program, to function better with what he has."

On the plus side, I had been breathing without mechanical assistance for the past six months. My vital capacity was markedly diminished, less than one fourth of normal, but adequate for normal breathing. What I lacked was the ability to draw a deep breath for coughing. To deal with that, I was taught a technique called glossopharyngeal breathing. Simply put, it is the process of pumping air into the lungs by gulping and pushing the tongue against the roof of the mouth like a bellows. It is commonly called "frog breathing" because the cheeks puff out when gulping air. I was told that the technique originated with pearl divers in the South Pacific who used it to expand their lungs so they could stay under water longer. It took a long time for me to get the hang of it but it proved to be a valuable tool for stretching the lungs and coughing. By pumping up, I can increase lung capacity to at least half of normal, a big increase.

The first step towards more function was sitting up straight in the wheelchair. Sitting upright, I could move my trunk forward and back through a combination of head movements and the few remaining back muscles at my command. They were weak but adequate for the task. So, the back of my chair was raised and the head rest removed. A foam cushion was used to pad my skinny behind. A lapboard was slipped over the chair arms so I could rest my arms and hands, no more dangling in my lap.

Sitting up straight without a full compliment of muscles required a corset to keep the spine from bending or twisting. At Warm Springs I was fitted with a new corset, a body brace made from fabric with Velcro straps. For added stability two metal stays were fastened on the back, parallel to the spine. I had been fitted with a metal and leather back brace at St. Joe's, but it inflicted rope burns under my arms and pit marks on my hips. It was inflexible and uncomfortable; I couldn't sit in it for long. The Warm Springs model was much lighter but still adequate to hold my trunk upright. It was also easier to get on and off. I was able to sit up for longer and longer periods with my new corset. I had no further use for a reclining wheelchair; a new one was ordered without a reclining back. It was more compact for easier turning and it took up less space when stored in the trunk of a car.

One improvement always led to another. The corset allowed the staff to use a different method of transferring to and from the bed or a car seat. They called it a "plus one" transfer. Instead of one or two people lifting me by the neck and knees, one person could transfer me safely without bearing my full weight. To do this the person faced me and straddled my knees with his while I placed my chin on his shoulder. By gripping the bottom of the corset and rocking back, I could be lifted and pivoted safely to the chair or to the bed, or to the seat of a car. The staff expected me to use it and teach it to every one of my future caregivers. With a little practice I was comfortable with this procedure and I've used it ever since. On occasion, I've instructed total strangers how to transfer me safely.

The pace of rehabilitation seemed to quicken with every passing day. I was pushed to daily physical therapy sessions with Berle Hambidge. In addition to stretching exercises, the staff ordered long leg braces and crutches from the brace shop. I was wheeled there many times for proper fitting. Standing was considered very important for circulation and maintaining bone strength. At St. Joseph's, I had used a standing board, a table with a foot board at a right angle. Once strapped to it, the table could be tilted to a standing position. In Warm Springs, the staff thought that standing with leg braces and crutches was more beneficial. The pressure under the arms from the crutches served to put the spine and the hips in proper alignment, and the heel cords could be stretched more thoroughly.

Berle and an aide helped with the standing exercise. When I mentioned it in a letter, Mom thought progress was being made, that I was actually going to walk. I wish! The few weak muscles scattered about my body were as good as it would get. I was well aware of the permanency of my paralysis. I just laughed, "No Mom, you wouldn't believe how strapped up my legs and arms are. There is even a little device to hook the braces together at the bottom. This is purely exercise."

Standing alone was a matter of balance. My crutches were well-padded under the armpits and my hands were belted into a grip in the middle. I could stand in a tripod position if the crutches were placed properly. Standing there I had enough muscle to get into trouble but not enough to get back out. If I wiggled my butt too much I was in danger of losing that delicate balance. One day I noticed something new in the full-length mirror in front of me. I had grown in the past year. The added height wasn't beneficial but I was no longer a boy. When I finally topped out at six foot and three inches, I was tied with Uncle Nick as the tallest member of the family.

Physical therapy was only one facet of the rehab process. The occupational therapist helped make better use of the most important piece of equipment I have: my mouthstick. The one I used at St. Joe's, a wooden dowel with a rubber tip on one end and a rubber sleeve on the other, put great strain on the jaw muscles, thereby limiting its usefulness. The occupational therapy staff used dental plastic to create a custom mouthpiece. It spread the weight evenly on my front teeth and anchored it to several of the back teeth. The mouthpiece was fitted to a bracket to which the wooden dowel was attached. Finally, I had something that was comfortable to use. Sitting upright I could lean forward and turn my head from side to side. Suddenly I could push books around on the lapboard, turn pages, dial a telephone, flip switches, type or manage anything else that I could reach with the stick.

A new appointment was added to the schedule with the arrival of my new wheelchair. A push-boy wheeled me to Roosevelt Hall where most of the therapeutic exercises took place, but this time no crutches or leg braces were involved. I was introduced to Mr. James Poulson, upper-arm orthotics expert. I had no idea what that meant but I liked Jim Poulson from the beginning. He was a slender man with big glasses and a kindly grin, dressed in white, and seated in a wheelchair. I could see the long leg braces peeking out from under his trouser legs. I had seen him exercising on several occasions and assumed he was another patient. Stricken with polio after his stint in the army in the late '40s, Jim left his native Ohio for rural Georgia and a life of helping other polio victims.

"We call them 'feeders' here at Warm Springs," Jim told me. "I'm going to fit you with feeders for your arms." I didn't know what he was talking about but I was curious. When I asked him what these feeders would do for me, he said, "Dick, feeders can be your ticket to the dining hall, and more." From that point forward, he had my complete attention and cooperation.

I soon learned that feeders were mechanical devices consisting of ball bearings, metal rods, and metal cradles for the arms. Jim's job was to configure these devices in such a way as to harness my few remaining upper body muscles. He was convinced that I could use weak head and trunk movement, some shoulder shrugging ability, and a feeble bicep in the right arm to feed myself with these adaptive devices. If nothing else, the feeders would help me sit up straight, allow me to work my arms back and forth, and keep them from getting sore on the lapboard. The elevation would also keep the fingers from turning purple.

The process of finding the proper length of each of the two rods, the proper angle of the bearings, and the correct fit for the cradles was very time-consuming. A different approach for each arm was necessary because the muscles were different on each side. However, Jim was a very patient and analytical man. On occasion, he would simply sit in his wheelchair, pipe in hand, studying the situation. He told me that others were convinced that building feeders was a simple matter of applying physics and engineering to the process. Jim and his team from Warm Springs were often confronted at conferences by people from other rehabilitation institutions who utilized the erudite scholarship of mechanical engineers. "We were often called those 'twisters and benders from Georgia,'" he related with a grin. "However, the difference between their feeders and ours is that ours work."

Jim Poulson was a master at analyzing weak muscles for functionality. After some quiet study and a few puffs on his pipe, he would say, "I think we can harness this muscle for something useful." Then he would reach into his ever-present bag of parts and pull out a particular piece. He had rods of different lengths, bearings set at different angles, and several types of swiveling mechanisms. In true trial-and-error fashion, he arranged these parts in different combinations, hoping that I might overcome the twin evils of gravity and inertia to bring my hands from the lapboard to my mouth and back again. After setting up a particular combination, he would say, "How does that work?" If it didn't, he might bend or twist a piece and ask again. It was slow and repetitive work. Sometimes, he would just stop. "We don't want to make bad worse. How tired are you?"

I learned that it was best to give an honest answer. "Well, I'm pretty tired."

"Then we'll wait until tomorrow."

The next day he would bend something else, twist something else. This process went on for months. Gradually, all the bending and twisting started to work. Jim harnessed the bit of bicep muscle in the right arm to pull my right hand toward my body. From there I could bring the hand up to my mouth by leaning forward slightly and pushing down with a weak shoulder muscle. I took it back down by leaning backwards. Presto, it was the motion necessary to feed myself. By attaching a combination fork and spoon (called a "spork") on a swivel to the bar on which my hand rested, and putting a backstop called a plate guard around the plate, I was ready for action. With practice and some fine-tuning, I mastered the art of transferring food from plate to mouth without slinging it over my shoulder.

The left arm presented more of a challenge. I had no muscle in that arm at all, just some shoulder twitches and trunk movement. Yet, a functioning feeder on that side was necessary for proper balance. When it was time to give my right arm a rest, Jim would turn to the left side. The left hand was fitted with a splint to keep the wrist straight. He warned me after weeks of struggle that the left arm would never function like the right but he was determined to get the same down and out, up and in, motion so necessary for balance and range. He did. Although the left side had limited function, I could move the arm up and down. In time, I learned to use it to hold my mouthstick, or balance a sandwich on top of the fist while I nibbled on it.

I practiced with the feeders at every opportunity. Before long I was in them every moment I spent in the wheelchair. Jim and the occupational therapy staff crafted a device to hold a pen on the right side and with some effort I learned to write. I lacked the fine motor skill necessary to do it with the feeder alone so I started using my mouthstick to guide the feeder. That combination worked well. Mostly I used it for my signature or to write brief notes, but being able to do these ordinary things built some self-confidence, some sense of well-being.

Being able to write meant I could sign papers and take control of my checking account again, even though there was nothing in it. Being able to feed myself was a great morale builder. It was embarrassing to be fed; anything that allowed me to be less dependent on others was a boost in self-esteem. I felt a great sense of accomplishment when I was allowed to return to the dining hall. The waiter cut up the portions and put the guard around the back of the plate and I took it from there. The long straws from the occupational therapy department made it possible to drink liquids at my own pace. Jim Poulson's skill and patience had paid great dividends.

Being in his charge also gave me access to some of the locals who worked in the shop where the adaptive devices were made. They created a wide variety of adaptive equipment, custom fitted to each patient's needs. Jim worked closely with them as they built my feeders from his prototypes. I could tell they had great respect for each other. It was a bond forged by a common desire to make life better for people like me.

The bond was strong enough to overcome a big difference in attitude towards race. Like so many others from the North who worked there, Jim must have accepted segregation as the price for doing what he loved to do. Although he never spoke directly, I sensed that Jim was quietly sympathetic when telling the story of the New Yorker who arrived in Warm Springs for equipment repair with his black caregiver. When told that his helper couldn't eat with him in the dining hall, the man said "I'll eat where he does," and they both ate in the kitchen.

The fellows in the brace shop had a different twist to the story. They told me the guy just "didn't understand the way things are down here." Well, I didn't understand either. How could a black person prepare your meals or wash your private parts and not be allowed to sit next to you on a bus or share your dinner table? It seemed to me that this "institution" should have been laughed out of existence long ago. I wasn't aware that segregation was mandated by state and local law throughout the South. When the civil rights movement exploded on the scene in the next decade, I finally understood the true meaning of what I had witnessed.

Hanging around the brace shop gave me some opportunity to explore white Southern culture. The brace shop guys were country folk with a rich oral history. The Civil War was still very meaningful to them. My ancestors immigrated after the war and the stories I was told related to blizzards, droughts, and the Great Depression. These guys had heard stories about Sherman's march through Georgia and the burning of Atlanta. They were also aware of Northern attempts to force them to accept former slaves as equals. To them, anyone not born or raised in the South couldn't possibly understand the ordeal they'd been put through. The "Damn Yankee" epitaph was thrown around quite frequently, mostly in good humor. When it was thrown at me, I objected. "I'm no Yankee; Nebraska didn't become a state until 1867, two years after the war. I'm a Westerner." At the time, I didn't know that the Nebraska Territory contributed 3,300 men to the Union cause. Fortunately for me, they didn't either.

Happily, my educational opportunities in Warm Springs weren't limited to back room banter with the brace shop guys. I was enrolled in a special school as well. I took two courses: American History and English Grammar. Although not as colorful or vivid in detail as the oral history taught in the brace shop, my History textbook was more objective.

I had regularly scheduled visits with the staff psychologist during my stay. Like Jim Poulson, she too was in a wheelchair, another polio survivor. She lived independently in one of the nearby cottages. My visits with her were enjoyable and productive. She stressed the positives, telling me often that the key to the future was education and perseverance. To emphasize the point that my brain was fully functioning, she administered an intelligence test. It was good enough to stoke my ego but I've forgotten the score.

While all this was happening, Berle Hambidge decided it was time to add another element to my physical therapy. It was time to exercise in the pool. The 88 degree mineral spring water that gave Warm Springs its name was piped into an indoor pool, the outdoor one used by FDR had been abandoned. Exercising in warm water was relaxing and the buoyancy made it possible for weakened muscles to function more normally. At least that was the theory. I had my doubts about this. I am a "flatlander" from a prairie state who never learned to swim before polio. Two inches of water in a bathtub was sufficient for me, and I didn't have that many muscles to exercise.

But Berle insisted. So, dressed in my swimming trunks, I was escorted by the push-boys to my newest adventure. Berle had exchanged her customary white uniform for a bathing suit and was waiting for me in the pool. The ever present pool aides hoisted me over the side and into her arms. Later, they would haul me out again. The water was four feet deep or so and there were other patients and therapists splashing about. Wooden exercise tables and chairs were bolted to the floor. She floated me to a table. With my head on a built-in headrest, my nose and mouth were safely above the water. Once the fear of imminent drowning subsided, I enjoyed the sensation of being in the water. I could actually move my limbs somewhat because of the water's buoyancy as she stretched my arms and legs. Sitting in the wooden chair was not so relaxing; my arms and legs had a tendency to float off.

I don't recall how long each session lasted or how often I was taken to the pool room. But, as a replacement for the ordinary stretching and bending routine, it was a welcome opportunity to exercise longer without fatigue. Nothing short of a miracle would return any muscle to normal but the water helped develop stamina, the stamina necessary to use the feeders for longer periods.

All of the pieces were now in place; my functional program was fully functional. This was as good as it would get for me physically. The occupational therapy staff did have one last surprise. They created a special mouthstick for picking up small things that worked surprisingly well. I called it a "pincher mouthstick." It was a long slim metal tube with a set of delicate jaws at the lower end. A stiff wire was attached to the moveable jaw, threaded through the tube, and attached to a mouthpiece fitted for my lower teeth. An upper mouthpiece was permanently attached to the upper end of the tube. I could open and close the jaws by thrusting my jaw forward and back. It turned out to be very useful for recreational activities like playing cards, or for putting paper in my typewriter.

Five months had passed since my entry into this sanctuary. The terrified boy mired in hopelessness and helplessness was gone and a young man with an array of adaptive devices had emerged. I wasn't yet an "alpha" male but I was equipped both physically and psychologically to cope with my situation. It was time to go home. The prospect both excited and saddened me. It would be wonderful to be with my family again and see the wide-open spaces of my native Nebraska, but Warm Springs had become my home as well. I had learned so much in such a short time. I was surrounded by capable and caring staff and had shared experiences with others in similar situations. It was a community where I felt secure. I vowed to return someday after completing my education. Inspired by Jim Poulson and the staff psychologist, I thought that I too could contribute something.

The folks were asked to come down a few days before my release date to get familiar with my new equipment and routines. I was told that regular outpatient visits would be necessary to insure that my devices remained in good condition and were working well in real life. I did so when possible over the years; my last visit was in 1997.

The years have not been kind to the Georgia Warm Springs Foundation. The crown jewel in the fight against polio was no longer necessary; the fight had been won. Salk's vaccine had stopped the terrible epidemics, and the March of Dimes turned its attention to birth defects. The State of Georgia took over funding after the March of Dimes dropped its affiliation. Today, the place has been renamed the Roosevelt Warm Springs Institute for Rehabilitation and it serves the people of that region, black and white alike. The emphasis today is on all kinds of paralysis from disease to spinal injuries.

For me, it will always remain the magic kingdom where I regained my self-confidence and sense of purpose. Life at home would be sedate after all that activity in Warm Springs. Many years would pass before I could re-capture that magic in the real world. I threw up again on the train ride home.

Home from Warm Springs with our rat terrier.

7

Superintendent Andersen

My experience at Warm Springs taught me one essential fact: my paralysis was permanent. No therapy or exercise would repair the nerve damage caused by polio; what little muscle remained could be harnessed for minimal function only. The emphasis throughout my stay had centered on the motto, "Use what you got." An inventory revealed the obvious: what I had was my mind and my mouth. I was encouraged to further my education. Where it might lead, nobody could say, but it was the only positive option in a field full of negatives. Education was my only hope for the future.

Upon my return in May of 1957, after nearly two years of rehabilitation, I was the forgotten man. My high school class was graduating and moving on; the boy who had spent two years with them was also gone. It was as if I'd died. The only thing missing was the picture with the black border in the yearbook. In fact, one of the few classmates who did remain in touch with me through the years was told at a class reunion that I had died.

"That's funny," said my friend, "I just visited him recently; he looked fine to me."

My education to date had taken several paths. I spent several early grades in a country school within a mile of the family farm. It was a one-room schoolhouse without indoor plumbing; eight grades of students learning together under a single teacher. Each class in turn recited their lessons at her big desk in the front of the room. I had one classmate. In addition to studying my own assignments, I could listen to other classes getting their instructions.

"Town" school was a big change. Instead of one classmate, I found myself in the company of many. The nuns at Guardian Angels School, both grade school and high school, drilled us in the fundamentals of learning and religious education, the primary reason for me being there. After grade school and two years of high school, I was well-schooled in spelling, punctuation, grammar, and the basics of math—the foundation for any higher learning. But the journey had been interrupted by polio; I was two years shy of the necessary credits for graduation.

Graduation from high school was no longer a mere prelude to a farming career; the bar was now set much higher. We were never contacted by the parochial school teachers or staff about future educational opportunities. Perhaps they had nothing further to offer. For one thing, the physical barriers that existed for moving a wheelchair in and out were formidable if not impossible. In the 1950s there was no emphasis on removing physical barriers or on "mainstreaming" students with disabilities.

My parents turned to the Cuming County public school system for help. The Superintendent, R.C. Andersen, told them the public high school would have the same problem accepting a student in a wheelchair. However, he readily agreed that I should be pushed down the path of education. Furthermore, he offered to do the pushing himself.

Thus began my return to formal education, with a private tutor no less. Mr. Andersen came to the farm twice a week for about two hours at a time. Considering all the obligations he had as superintendent of a county-wide school system, it must have been a real sacrifice for him. However, Mr. Andersen loved the art of learning, the pursuit of knowledge for its own sake. He was a great believer in the power of language. According to Mr. Andersen, the best way to release that power was to read, read, and read some more. He spoke of his own experience with his son, Robert. Mr. Andersen said, "I couldn't get him interested in reading until he discovered comic books. I decided that reading comic books was better than reading nothing so I bought lots of comic books." He was so proud that Robert had gone on to become a doctor.

I needed no prodding when it came to reading. Books had become my refuge following polio. I spent hours reading in bed, using a special reading board designed by a local carpenter and my mouthstick to turn the pages. I had become an avid reader, devouring everything Mom brought from the public library. Mr. Andersen brought discipline into the equation. He had limited time to spend with me and that required self preparation in order to respond to his questions. He used the formal student-teacher routine as much as possible. We didn't have a blackboard but he brought a big music stand to prop up his lesson plan. Mostly we

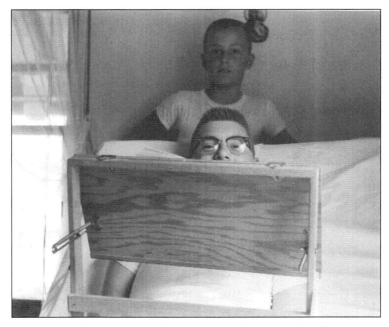

Reading in bed with a little help from my brother

concentrated on social studies. I was surprised to learn recently that Mr. Andersen taught Algebra I and General Mathematics at the high school; we did not cover physics, chemistry or math. I had taken two years of algebra in parochial school; perhaps he thought that was sufficient. My studies were broken into categories; he gave reading assignments as we worked our way through textbooks in each subject area. Since I enjoyed reading, it was easy for me to do large amounts of independent study. As for written homework, he would give whatever he thought my mother could tolerate. She was my writing hand in those days.

Mr. Andersen went over homework and presented lessons just as any teacher would do in a classroom. He utilized the necessary drilling and rote memorization component of education. However, he also saw the opportunity to indulge in the process of learning whereby the instructor asks question after question, the Socratic Method. I was subjected to question and answer sessions repeatedly. To respond accurately, I had to know the subject matter and defend my position. Given Mr. Andersen's inquisitive nature, these sessions covered a wide range of topics. Because of preparation and a good memory, I could hold my own, mostly. On more than one occasion, he told my mother: "That's my boy! I only wish my other students had his dedication." If only he knew how much I wished I could be more like his other students. They had options. Dedication comes easy when there are no options.

During my time at home, I spent a good part of each morning in bed. A typical day included reading, preparing my lessons, and exercise. Mom did all of the necessary personal hygiene every morning. Dad got me out of bed and into the wheelchair around noon. On evenings not committed to Mr. Andersen, we continued the exercises I was given at Warm Springs, especially the standing exercise. After strapping on the leg braces and the crutches, Dad hoisted me to my feet and helped me find my balance. One night, I wiggled too much and lost that balance. As I toppled towards the floor, Dad grabbed the safety belt around my waist but it was too late; the best he could do was prevent a hard landing. I had never fallen before. The shock turned to laughter with the discovery that nothing was broken.

Mr. Andersen was my first teacher in the fine art of arguing or discussing events with people. He once told me: "People are much too reticent to discuss things unless they are confronted directly. For example, if you ask somebody 'What do you think of President Eisenhower?' he will give you a non-committal

My family in 1958. After hoisting me to a standing position, Dad has his hand on my safety belt, just in case.

answer like 'I don't know, or what do you think?' But if you say: 'Don't you agree that President Eisenhower is a real s.o.b.?' he will have to respond yes or no. From there you can have a real discussion." Mr. Andersen was a very interesting man indeed. I think most people in West Point were appreciative of his contributions, including his "discussions." As I remember, he was a big man but from a wheelchair everyone looks tall. Mr. Andersen opened the door to higher education for me. I'm grateful that he lived long enough to see his efforts rewarded.

After two years of tutelage, Mr. Andersen announced "You have completed the high school curriculum and you are eligible for a diploma." I don't recall his criteria for coming to that conclusion but it sounded good to me. He added, "If you had been in school, you would have ranked 1st or 2nd in the class, but I don't think

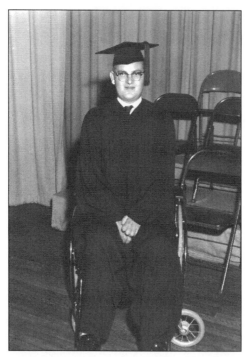

**Graduate of West Point High 1959. I swore I would
never wear another cap & gown.**

that would be fair to them, so I am going to rank you 3rd." My
rank didn't make any difference to me, I was happy to graduate.

I was still conscious of my disability and my wheelchair and
had no desire to take part in the graduation ceremony. However,
my parents insisted that I participate and Mr. Andersen made
sure that I had a cap and gown. A few students from the high
school came to the house to visit me before graduation, but other
than that, graduation was the first time I met most of my
classmates. I was wheeled onto the stage for graduation as a
member of the graduating class of 1959, 33 members strong. My
picture was placed in the yearbook along with the other seniors
above the caption: "He has his goal well in mind."

8

Uncle LeRoy & Aunt Joanie To The Rescue

The goal, of course, was higher education. During that difficult year in the polio ward at St. Joseph's Rehabilitation Center, I noticed that the two persons coping with disability the best were lawyers. In spite of their paralysis, they were not consumed by the disease. They were still interested in the activities taking place beyond the boundaries of the ward. I was the recipient of much information during their discussions of current events, and allowed to read their news magazines. This was too cool; I wanted to be like them. From that time forward, becoming a lawyer became my dream. However, I didn't know if the dream could ever become reality and was only vaguely aware of the education required. The obstacles were both obvious and vast.

Dad didn't put much stock in "book learning." Armed with an eighth grade education only, and the "hands on" training of his father, he had attained his dream of being a farmer. But, in his typical blunt assessment, he confided to a friend: "Dick's got to go to college because he can't do anything with his hands."

How true. My farming days were over. I might have had my goal well in mind, but getting there was another thing. Thanks to Mr. Andersen, I was a high school graduate; but getting money for college seemed like an insurmountable barrier. My parents incurred huge medical bills the year that my sister and I contracted polio, and they lost their crops as well because of a severe drought. In addition, cattle prices had fallen through the roof. Most of our farm machinery and vehicles had been sold to pay debts. The replacements were of lesser quality and barely adequate to continue operations. The idyllic farm life of my youth was gone forever, we were struggling financially. Where would we find money for college? I needed money for tuition and room and board as well as help for personal care and transportation.

While we searched for a way to finance my education, my spirits were lifted continually by my extended family. The future is forged in the past; my past is replete with caring and gentle family members. I am truly blessed by the foundation that was laid for me. Family gatherings or visits were the setting for board games, cards, sing-alongs, or lively conversation. I was a welcome member of this clan, secure in the knowledge that I was loved and accepted.

For two years, my family tried in vain to find funding for college. One possible source was the Vocational Rehabilitation Act. It provided federal money to disabled people for educational training but funds were limited. The area supervisor charged with distributing the funds did not consider me a good investment. How could a young man so physically impaired possibly have the stamina to complete college, much less be employed? Funds were better spent where there was less risk of failure and a better return for the dollar.

No one stepped forward to break the logjam; no one that is, but my Uncle LeRoy and his wife, Joanie. Uncle LeRoy, Mom's only brother, is six years older than I. Growing up, he was a big brother of sorts. As a youngster, I was allowed to spend a lot of time at Grandma Johnson's house on South Monitor Street in West Point. Many times I returned home with cuts, bumps and bruises; Uncle played rough, but it was always a grand adventure. Uncle LeRoy and his dog, Spanky, occupied the bedroom at the top of the stairs. There was usually mischief afoot there and many things to explore. Uncle was always building or playing with something interesting, something that shocked, or stunk, or was worse. I think I was his guinea pig for pranks that he would later play on his sisters.

As time passed, I saw less and less of my aunts Donna and Beverly during my visits. They were busy with high school activities and making plans for the future. The bedroom at the end of the hall belonged to them; I don't recall ever being invited into their sanctuary. I think the novelty of having a nephew had worn off and they regarded me as a younger version of their brother.

Uncle LeRoy also spent hours on the farm with us and worked for Dad during the summers. My grandfather died when Uncle was only five and Grandma Johnson thought he should stay busy and have a male role model. It was a help for us and a help for her. My parents paid him when they could, but mostly he returned home with eggs, meat, liver or vegetables.

For Dad, farming was the only way of life; Uncle had other thoughts. Even though he spent a great deal of time on the farm, Uncle had grown up living in town. He had been exposed to other ideas and other ways of life. While Dad talked about how wonderful it was to be independent, Uncle was not so enthusiastic. He had seen the financial ups and downs and the grind of daily chores. Uncle loved the outdoors for hunting, hiking, or camping, not farming. Leaning on his shovel in the hog pen one day, he remarked to me: "It's hard to consider yourself free and independent when you're ankle-deep in hog manure."

Uncle LeRoy's first visit to St. Joe's.

The world Uncle LeRoy left behind when he enlisted in the army in 1953 lay in tatters upon his return. Instead of an active teenager eagerly awaiting his tales of military life, he found a helpless invalid wasting away in Omaha. Although I'm sure my parents warned him what to expect, our reunion must have been gut-wrenching for him. I don't remember anything about the visit; I do remember shedding a few tears after he and the folks left for home.

Uncle LeRoy continued to work on the farm during the summers after his return, but his future lay elsewhere. He enrolled at the State University of South Dakota under the GI Bill. He also fell in love. Like me, my soon-to-be Aunt Joanie attended Guardian Angels High School. She was two grades ahead of me and undoubtedly less than impressed with that impudent Wieler boy.

After the marriage, Uncle and Joanie made their summer home at the old house on the farm. It had been empty since our last hired man was released. They also drove home from South Dakota on the weekends during the school year to help out when it was necessary. During this period, Joanie and Mom became good friends and they talked often about my situation over coffee in the kitchen. My stock with her had risen dramatically since our high school days together. Although I never saw Mom cry over me, I am told that she shed many tears of frustration during those talks.

In the spring of 1961, Uncle LeRoy graduated from the State University of South Dakota with a master's degree in Mathematics. Unbeknownst to us, Lockheed Aircraft offered him a job in one of their engineering groups. No doubt he would have made a substantial amount of money had he taken it. The University also offered him a teaching position in the Physics department. He and Joanie decided he would take the university job, and forgo Lockheed and the money.

They wanted to play a part in my struggle and they had a plan. Uncle reasoned that rehabilitation funds would become more available if I proved I could do college work, and nothing was being accomplished sitting at home. "Look," Uncle LeRoy said, "The only way we are going to prove anything is if he goes to college!" They invited me to live with them and their new baby, my cousin Jim, and enroll at the State University of South

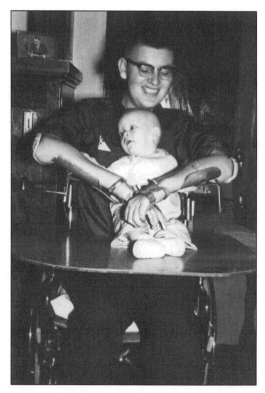

**Cousin Jimmie: Can you believe this baby
grew up to be my caretaker for a year?**

Dakota. My parents and I were elated. A door to the future was being unlocked.

Grandma Johnson was part of the plan. I am sure that she was the first one to volunteer to help. Perhaps no one ever set a better example of a life well spent than our Grandma Johnson. Known to family and friends alike as "Grandma John," she taught us how to face life's challenges with courage and optimism. In her own quiet way, she faced life's storms without losing faith in the rainbow or the silver lining. The loss of a child, their farm and then, her husband, and later, several young grandchildren, could not diminish her strength, or blunt her enjoyment of life. Grandma John was devoted to her family. After her children had homes of their own, she kept their homes running during family emergencies and traveled from place to place as the need arose. She would see to my personal care in South Dakota. When told of this arrangement, the area supervisor agreed to spend Vocational Rehabilitation funds for tuition and books.

Uncle LeRoy and Aunt Joanie had been living in a converted garage, but it was too small for my needs. They decided to rent a big house that would be large enough for lots of people. In addition to Grandma and me, they planned to offer rooms on the upper level to college students in exchange for their help. The students would be a valuable safety net in case something came up that Uncle couldn't handle. The students were to help me get to and from classes. One of their biggest responsibilities would be the task of dealing with stairs on a campus that was not fully accessible. Without much effort, Uncle was able to find several young men who accepted the

Grandma Johnson: Our family treasure

arrangement for room only. Food was not part of the package; our combined budget was too tight.

Our new dwelling was certainly big enough but in need of some major housecleaning. It was a challenge for Mom and Aunt Joanie to make it livable. They spent hours scrubbing it. My aunt and uncle bought ten items of furniture on sale for $200. They didn't have the money to buy it outright so they made payments. Uncle also built a ramp to the ground floor because the house wasn't accessible. With all the pieces in place, it was time to put the plan into action. I was enrolled in college at last.

9

Adventure In South Dakota

The State University of South Dakota was located in Vermillion, South Dakota, a hundred miles from West Point and a universe away from the farm. During my first week there, Uncle LeRoy and I took a walking tour of the campus. Although the grounds were level and there were wide sidewalks everywhere, most of the buildings were not readily accessible. It was probably typical of most campuses before accessibility was mandated by subsequent federal legislation. We knew we'd have to deal with steps at some point during each school day. In the midst of our tour, a man approached and patted me on the shoulder. Saying how sorry he was about my condition, the guy put a dollar in my shirt pocket.

Arriving back at the house, we told everybody about our encounter. Mom was still there helping to get the house in shape; she was quite offended that someone would think I was an object of charity. "Oh, that's so embarrassing! What did you say to him?"

"I just thanked him, and told him I wished he had more. After all, I'm now a poor college student."

On that note, I was ready to begin my career at the State University of South Dakota. The University's mascot is the coyote. Although it doesn't occupy a lofty spot on the predator chain, the coyote is tough, resourceful, and able to adapt to changes in its environment. Because of that, it survives where others have not. As I look back, the coyote was a perfect symbol for the traits I needed to develop to deal with the challenges that confronted me. It was the fall of 1961, and at age 21 I was about to return to a regular classroom for the first time since the end of my sophomore year in high school.

One of the challenges was transportation. Being transferred to and from a car and the wheelchair was time consuming; each transfer made me more uncomfortable. On top of that, Uncle LeRoy's first new car was a Chevrolet Corvair, Detroit's first compact vehicle. The Corvair had a short shelf life after Ralph Nader trashed it in his book *Unsafe at any Speed,* but Uncle loved it. However, it took both strength and courage to stuff me into the front seat of that car. To solve this problem, Dad bought a well-used laundry delivery van. He and Uncle built a portable ramp and mounted the winch from Uncle's boat trailer behind the driver's seat to pull the chair up the ramp. Cargo straps were used to hold the wheelchair in place inside. We were quite pleased with ourselves for rigging up such a system. It wasn't very pretty but it was all we could afford at the time. There was only one problem: the vehicle wouldn't start most of the time. Our system worked, but the van did not.

That little truck seemed to have a mind of its own. Where was Ralph Nader when we really needed him? All year we tried to get it to run consistently. Mostly, it sat in the backyard waiting for Uncle's attempts at auto repair. Once, while he was tinkering under the hood, he stood up suddenly and gave the front tire a vicious kick. When he saw me grinning at him, he said "Stop laughing. It makes *me* feel better!"

We used it when we could. One frosty night, Uncle LeRoy and I took the van to see the basketball game against our archrival South Dakota State. Aunt Joanie didn't join us. Like Dad, she couldn't understand how grown men could spend perfectly good money to watch a basketball game. Anyway, the trip to the gym was uneventful, but after the game the van wouldn't start. In utter frustration and lacking other alternatives, Uncle pushed me back home.

So much for transportation plan A; we switched to plan B. It was less frustrating for Uncle LeRoy, or the guys living with us, to simply push me the three blocks to campus. It became routine. Grandma washed me in the morning, Uncle LeRoy put me in the wheelchair, and he or the guys pushed me to campus. We coordinated our schedules so someone was available to get me to my classes, and to lift the wheelchair up and/or down the stairs where necessary.

This routine worked very well during those pleasant autumn months. However, winter arrived early and stayed late that year. We dealt with heavy snowfall most of the season. I've been told that snowfall totals in February alone were the most recorded in the region since records were first kept in 1890. I just remember having to deal with mounds of snow. Aunt Joanie sums it up this way: "It was a long winter of snow shoveling and cabin fever." It seemed to snow every weekend. We struggled to get our weekly groceries; Joanie got so tired of being housebound that she bundled baby Jim up and walked through snow drifts just to visit friends.

Everybody was having great difficulty negotiating the clogged streets; the van may have been of some help had it chosen to run. Our solution was to make a dog sled out of the wheelchair. Using a long rope tied to the front of the chair, two of the guys pulled and Uncle LeRoy pushed the three blocks from the house to the campus. Once a path was shoveled to the street, the chair could be forced through the drifts or piles of snow left by the snowplows. We must have been quite a sight, mushing up the middle of the street.

My first class that winter was an English class. The building was accessible but the classroom had an uneven floor that slanted towards the front of the room. I could hear the snow melting off my wheelchair as I sat there. By the time the hour was over, water was pooling at the instructor's feet.

Other buildings were not as accessible. The guys negotiated flights of stairs by tipping the wheelchair back on its large rear wheels and "rocking" it backwards up one step at a time. Going down stairs was another matter. We used the same technique, tipping the chair on its back wheels, but went down forward rather than backward. Going down was much scarier.

Several classes were located in a building with a short flight of steps at the rear entrance. However, we couldn't easily exit that way because of the large number of students entering the building and because those steps were slippery when wet. The best solution was to use a longer inside stairs to another exit. This required two helpers; one gripping the handles on the back of the wheelchair and the other grabbing the front foot pedals. We bumped down the stairs one step at a time with the chair on its rear wheels. Facing forward, I had a clear view of the steepness of the descent and the area below. I could also see a large African elephant head mounted on the wall across from the stairs on the floor below.

The task of handling the front end of the wheelchair belonged to Ren Whitaker. Unlike my other helpers, Ren wasn't recruited for the job, and he didn't live at the house. I met him in a German class; he volunteered to push me to another class because my other helpers had class conflicts. That chance meeting led to friendship and, on one occasion, may have saved my life.

We were still very near the top of the stairs when the helper in the back lost his grip and released the wheelchair. Ren felt the slip and knew he couldn't hold me in place. He started running backwards as fast as he could to keep the chair on its rear wheels and me from tipping forward. World War I veterans often referred to combat as "having seen the elephant." I saw the elephant that day; he was staring at me from his post on the wall as I was bouncing down the stairs. I wondered how long Ren could maintain this pace, how long the wheelchair could take the pounding, and what would happen to me if the answers to those questions were less than positive.

The wondering stopped swiftly when my other helper recovered and grabbed the wheelchair with one arm and the railing with the other. Somehow, Ren saw that coming too, and he was able to adjust to the sudden stop after being in free fall for three or four steps. As I remember, not a word was spoken during the entire event, just plenty of heavy breathing afterwards. Two days later, we were back on those stairs; classes were still on.

My approach to class work was also based on trial and error. I thought my writing techniques were too slow and clumsy to take notes in class. At first I experimented with a battery-powered tape recorder attached to the tray on my wheelchair. The idea was to allow me to review the lecture later and make notes at my own pace. I soon realized that this meant listening to the lecture twice; it was boring and repetitive. Instead, I asked other students if I could copy or even buy their notes. No problem! Although the notes were sometimes inconsistent, (it's hard to find the "A" students all the time) they helped jog my memory for exams. More importantly I discovered it was more beneficial to read the textbooks carefully, and to listen attentively in class. In fact, I listened so carefully that I never asked questions. It became a habit that I kept throughout my college years.

To make important notes or to write college papers, I used an electric IBM typewriter at home. Great-Aunt Effie had given it to me as a high school graduation present. I typed with my mouthstick, one key at a time. Oh, for the convenience of today's computer word processors; whiteout was my only friend. Thankfully, it was built into that model of typewriter, and I could activate it myself. Any mistakes or changes too large for whiteout meant typing the whole paper over again. It didn't take long to realize that I had to organize my thoughts before typing.

Also, my typing skills weren't bad; I could maintain twenty words a minute with few spelling errors.

Exams were another challenge. I asked my professors if I could take my exams orally. A few were agreeable, most were not. Oral exams were the easiest for me, and I think the professors who agreed to examine me orally got a kick out of it. Mr. Andersen had prepared me well for holding my own against tough questioning, and there was one other advantage. I could read the professor's face and see whether he was buying what I was saying, or if I needed to change direction or add more to make my point. For those who insisted on written exams, I asked if I could dictate to a helper who would transcribe my answers. At first, there seemed to be a concern about possible cheating but some monitoring resolved that. Again, no problem!

In the beginning, my joy at returning to the classroom was tempered by the fear that I would be seen as a freak or an object of pity. The time in Warm Springs and my years of tutoring with Mr. Andersen had restored a great deal of the sense of self-worth so ravished by polio, but I was still fearful of crowds. However, my relationship with the other students proved to be no problem. In spite of my adaptive equipment and lack of mobility, the students welcomed me into their community. We were there for the same purpose, education. Once they realized that I was seeking no special privileges and was willing to compete for grades on an equal footing, I became just another student.

Going to college became very manageable; I had both the time and the willingness to devote myself to the project. It meant establishing priorities and making sacrifices, but I was no longer a stranger to that. One burden was happily removed. At home my parents had continued the physical-therapy exercises I learned in Warm Springs. The exercises were supposedly designed to aid in blood circulation and to maintain strong bones, but I had come to doubt their value. In South Dakota, we stopped the daily therapy; it was not compatible with a busy academic schedule. Rather than spending several hours a day in therapy, I thought it more productive to use that time in study. It's a decision I've never regretted.

It was a busy year for all of us. Uncle LeRoy had to devote considerable time to his job as a fledgling professor. Grandma John devoted herself to my care and helping Joanie with household chores as well as looking after a lively two-year-old boy, and the newest addition to the household, a toy rat terrier pup named Pixie. Finances were tight but the food was fantastic. The folks chipped in with meat and produce from the farm, and Grandma and Joanie were always turning out pies and cookies. Grandma loved cookies! She always seemed to have one in her apron pocket when hungry grandchildren were near. We were able to return home for visits periodically, a task made much easier after Dad and Uncle swapped cars. Uncle LeRoy enjoyed zipping around town in his compact car, but Dad had a farmer's taste for bigger vehicles. Transferring into Dad's car was less arduous for me.

Our little commune functioned quite smoothly, all things considered. It was surely difficult at times for my aunt and uncle; they had little time to themselves. Although the house was big, they had to share some space with strangers who were living there for my benefit. It was not a normal environment for a young married couple with a child. For entertainment, we took advantage of the fact that there were four adults in the house. We played cards, mostly pinochle, but we also experimented with contract bridge. In addition, Uncle and I learned to play chess. Because we both hated losing, we spent hours staring at the board, studying possible moves and countermoves. It drove Aunt Joanie bananas; we were so absorbed at times that Uncle was ignoring her "honey-do" wishes. We finally quit by mutual consent after nearly missing turkey and dressing on Thanksgiving.

With our busy schedules, the months slipped by quickly. Winter's icy grip finally retreated and disappeared beneath spring's warm embrace, the commute to campus became pleasant again, and the school year drew to a close. My adventure in South Dakota had come to an end; I had completed twenty-six semester hours of college work. In those nine months in Vermillion, I had never been in the business district, or seen any part of the town, or the countryside beyond the campus. The Dean's office sent a letter of congratulations for finishing in the top 10% of the freshman class. I made the Dean's list both semesters, and I was initiated into the SUSD chapter of the National Freshman Honor Society, Phi Eta Sigma.

The sacrifice had paid off; we had proven our point! But would it be enough? Had we convinced the guardians of Vocational Rehabilitation funding that my education would be a good investment? Where would I find a college more accommodating to my needs? And most importantly, could I do it on my own, independently, without hands-on support from a loving family? Every success seemed to create new challenges.

Aunt Joanie and Uncle LeRoy years after coming to my rescue.

We threw a farewell party for all those who helped make the year a success. It was time to break up the commune; time for Uncle LeRoy, Aunt Joanie and little Cousin Jimmie to return to normal family life, and time for Grandma John to resume her family travels. As for me, the future was still out there somewhere, waiting.

10

College Student
Without A College

The summer of 1962 began in high spirits. After all, I had proven the point that I could do university work in South Dakota. Surely it would be a slam dunk to get into another program; it was just a matter of finding the right school. What a task that turned out to be. In those days there wasn't much emphasis on making college campuses accessible, or anything else accessible for that matter. The list of "right" schools known to us was quite small.

One possibility was a little college in Kansas, Emporia State College. The administration there had a sincere interest in making things accessible and the small campus reflected their efforts. I was impressed with the physical layout and the friendliness of the staff. However, the staff was concerned about my level of disability; they were convinced they would be unable to find adequate caretakers. I was not accepted.

We were also aware of the strides made privately at the University of Illinois in Champaign-Urbana. The folks and I were encouraged by my vocational rehabilitation counselor to visit the campus and speak with the administrator of their program. With some effort we made the trip by car, staying with Mom's sister and family in Indiana. What a disappointment! Although the campus was mostly level and many buildings had been modified for wheelchair use, I got the distinct impression that the administrator was more interested in finding paraplegics who could care for themselves. Actually, he seemed more interested in finding athletes to compete in the Special Olympics. I was told that my application could not be accepted at that time.

As other college students headed back to school that fall, I was back on the farm in the care of my parents. I was a college student without a college. It was extremely frustrating. The thrill of attending classes was replaced by the boredom of staring out the window. Had the year at the State University of South Dakota meant nothing? In my frustration, I wrote the following letter to the Omaha World-Herald Public Pulse:

> I am a quadriplegic, and have just returned from an unsuccessful attempt to enter the University of Illinois through its rehabilitation program.
> Although I maintained a 3.8 average out of a possible four through 26 hours of college work at the University of South Dakota last year, I was not accepted in Illinois because of the limited space and an overwhelming demand from handicapped people.
> As I will not be able to continue at the University of South Dakota, I face another two years of waiting before I can enter Illinois. This is just another set-back in my fight to get an education and become a useful member of society.

Although studies have proved that the cost of educating handicapped people for useful occupations and thus making them working, tax paying members of the community is far cheaper in the long run than having to maintain them as useless wards of the state, handicapped people still face public apathy, lack of funds and a limited number of institutions where they can receive an education.

With the need for professional knowledge and service ever rising, why are thousands of handicapped people, victims of disease and accidents, allowed to go to waste because of a lack of opportunity?

Richard Wieler, Jr.

The moniker "Junior" was given to me by Dad. It is traditional, and a good way to distinguish two people with the same name. However, it is not on my birth certificate and I chose to drop it in adulthood. I much preferred "Richard L.;" family and friends have always called me Dick.

Anyway, the letter was published by the World-Herald on September 6, 1962, the day of my grandfather's funeral. I can't say I knew my grandfather, Nicholas Wieler, very well. He and my father had their differences. I think grandfather felt obliged to hold Dad down somewhat, concerned about his ambitions and his big ideas about cattle feeding.

My grandfather succeeded the hard way. He lost his father while very young and quit school to help support his family. One of his first jobs was hauling hay to the Chicago stock yards. He left Illinois to seek his fortune on the prairies of Nebraska as a young adult. Hard work and wise investments certainly paid off;

Grandfather was able to accumulate three farms during the Great Depression.

All that happened before my time. I remember my grandfather as an old man bent over a cane. Most farmers have been hobbled one way or the other by chance encounters with livestock or farm machinery, encounters they invariably lose. Grandfather escaped that but was hurt in an automobile crash. The result left him badly impaired as he aged. He was always dressed in starched, white, long-sleeved shirts and moved slowly without complaint. Although I never heard him raise his voice, he seemed somewhat unapproachable. I never found the courage to ask him why he changed the family name from "Weiler" to "Wieler." Nobody else did either; it's still a mystery.

Grandfather died of leukemia. I'm told he refused further treatments when he was informed that the blood transfusions were only prolonging the process; there was no cure. He told the family of his decision and his wish to die at home. In fact, he put it quite bluntly: "If I wake up in a hospital, there will be hell to pay." Everybody believed him. Nobody reached for the phone when he lapsed into a coma.

On the day my grandfather's last chapter was completed, a new one opened for me. A woman in Gibbon, Nebraska, read my letter to the newspaper and responded to it immediately. Her letter was postmarked the next day and addressed only to Richard Wieler Jr., West Point, Nebraska. This is the text of her letter:

> Dear Richard,
>
> I read your letter in the Public Pulse and wanted you to know the Univ. of Missouri has a new department for

handicapped persons. My nephew tried also to get into the Univ. of Ill., but would have to wait until room was available. He learned of the Univ. of Mo. through a Doctor in Des Moines. He is a wheelchair patient & plans to enroll there this fall.

Good luck to you. With your determination, you will find success.

Very truly yours,
Mrs. John Ross

We contacted the University of Missouri immediately, and filled out the necessary applications. Then I waited, and waited. In the meantime, Mom scoured the library for books for me to read. As the school year slid by without me, and for lack of anything better to do, I took a four-hour correspondence course in plane geometry from the State University of South Dakota. I teased my uncle, the math major, that it was the first useful math course I had ever taken. It was practical stuff and could be applied to every day problems. I enjoyed the leisurely pace and the grade I got upon completion. However, it didn't do me any good academically because I discovered later that the credits were not transferable.

The winter of 1962 gave way to the spring of 1963. I passed my time at home, stuck in that all too familiar routine. But the memory of my year in South Dakota continued to lift my spirits. Any doubt about my ability to handle college courses had been crushed. Would the University of Missouri take notice and accept my application?

11

On My Own

The University of Missouri called in the late spring of 1963. I was eligible for enrollment that summer. We were stunned. Even my vocational rehabilitation counselor was elated by the news; he immediately approved the necessary funding for both college and caregiver services. Something important was happening here; my quest for an education was no longer a family matter.

The needs of the handicapped community were finally being addressed by society. A new federal law, The National Vocational Rehabilitation Act, had provided money for ten regional universities to make their campuses accessible. The University of Missouri in Columbia was selected as one of them. Campus renovation had started the year before, but it was still a work in progress. The program was attracting disabled students throughout the Midwest and the University was still struggling to properly assess and accommodate their needs.

Removing architectural barriers with ramps, wider doors, and elevators was only the first step. In the second year of the program, the University was in the process of establishing a workable counseling service and creating a clearinghouse where disabled students could exchange ideas and seek assistance. However, the school did find a young man to take care of me and I enrolled for seven credit hours that summer.

My folks packed my belongings and drove me to Columbia, the first of many trips over the years. We were introduced to my roommate-caregiver and gave him a crash course in my personal care. My home for the summer was Stafford Hall, an old dorm in the Pershing Group. Dorms were arranged in groups around a common dining hall. The dorms in Pershing Group looked like three-story barracks, functional but hardly awe inspiring. Although the upper two stories were not accessible, the ground floors were perfectly suitable for wheelchairs.

Like any other youngster headed off to college, I found myself in a whole new world, a world without family. There was one gigantic difference: I was paralyzed and in the care of a total stranger with only my mouth, my adaptive equipment, and my training from Warm Springs to get me through. Two things filled me with confidence: my earlier success with college course work, I was a sophomore after all, and my good health. I was paralyzed but my weight had returned to normal and my stamina was excellent. I could sit in my wheelchair from early morning until late at night without getting tired or sore. The prior stress-related ailments were a thing of the past.

For a monthly fee, the University provided a bus with a wheelchair lift to move handicapped students around the large campus, but its schedule never seemed to match mine and the lift broke constantly. Having had prior experience with balky vehicles, I found it easier to get pushed to my classes. I was learning quickly how to fend for myself, without family around and without a lot of backup. Upon arrival at my first class I came through the door asking classmates: "Are you taking General Experimental Psychology?" The first one who said "yes" was met with: "Good, I need a push to that building." From that time on I had a push to the other side of campus.

Life in the dorm was fantastic. I was surrounded by a good mix of handicapped and able-bodied students from different backgrounds and with different ambitions. As we got to know each other, a small community of the willing was established. The able-bodied guys (we called them "AB"s for short) were more than willing to help; I think they took great pride in our accomplishments. The banter was free and easy, as it should be among friends. Political correctness today would make that bonding process more difficult. To me, the "p.c." mania is ridiculous. I use the terms "handicapped" and "disabled" interchangeably but I'm told "disabled" is the correct term. I learned in the dorm that undue sensitivity is detrimental to developing relationships. Constantly offended people are irritating and they push people away who could become friends. I refuse to grant people the power to offend me with mere words; I still use the term "cripple" to describe myself. It's in the Bible.

Summer school at the University of Missouri was very exciting. I enjoyed my two courses and I picked up my first "C" in a college course. That was enough to keep me both humble and hungry. I survived that summer with no backup, no family, depending only on one helper and a few volunteers. I was no longer a South Dakota "Coyote," I was a Missouri "Tiger," a proud member of "Old Mizzou." My confidence was soaring. At the same time, I realized that I needed to be on familiar terms with many people to remain independent. The more people I knew, the better off I would be. One helper couldn't possibly be there at all times; after all, he was a student himself.

Before the summer semester was over, I found a new roommate-caregiver for the coming fall and winter semesters. That fall my base of operations moved to the ground floor of Defoe Hall, another dorm in the Pershing Group. We still ate at the same dining hall but Defoe was almost a block closer to the main campus. I was to spend the next three years in that old cinder-block building with some of the best dorm buddies a guy could ever hope to find. I had to lean on my new friends but they never seemed to mind. The guys were wonderful, a collection of upper classmen, one graduate student, and many freshmen, both able-bodied and handicapped. Every year brought in a new group to replace those who left and new friendships developed quickly. In the process of evaluating prospective helpers, I steadily improved my communication skills and the ability to deal with people.

Besides providing an accessible environment, the University's assistance to the disabled in those early years was limited, mostly assigning us to a dorm and helping with the initial enrollment process. After that, we were on our own. For me, it was another exercise in self-reliance. As in South Dakota, I made my own deals on testing with the professors. I explained my situation to them as soon as I could: "I can't write well enough to take an exam by myself. Can I do it orally?" Interestingly enough, one of the first to agree was the math instructor. Because my geometry correspondence course wasn't transferable, I needed a math course to meet the prerequisites for a BA degree. The course was called Basic College Algebra; taking the exams orally was quite different from any previous experience. It wasn't so bad working from the test papers that the instructor prepared for the class. However, when my helper pushed me into the classroom for the final, the instructor was standing by the blackboard, chalk in hand. For the next hour, it was a blur of problems and equations as I struggled to keep up with him. At one point, my helper got so engrossed that he jumped into the fray. For a few minutes the three of us were locked in algebraic mortal combat. "Surely this is cheating," I thought, but the instructor didn't seem to take notice. When it was finally over, I left the classroom exhausted. I got an "A" for my work but vowed never to take another math course.

Most of the professors said no to orals, but they were more than willing to consider other options. "Do you mind if my helper comes with me and writes out what I say?" That was my first option and the one usually agreed upon, with some monitoring to insure that I wasn't bringing an expert on the subject. When my caregiver was unavailable, I found someone else to help me with tests. Volunteers were always available in the dorm; it was simply a matter of asking the right person. My German professor was the greatest challenge. He refused to do oral exams and he wasn't keen on the idea of using a helper to write out my answers. He relented only with the assurance that my helper did not speak or understand German.

To insure passing grades, I had developed the habit of studying every day except one each week in South Dakota. That day off was a welcome relief valve from the rigors of study. Although there were more distractions in Missouri, I was determined to stick to that schedule. I knew instinctively that good grades were essential to my future. I read my assignments regularly, underlined passages in the text, made notes in the margins, and reviewed or copied notes I borrowed from other students. Although I felt my writing skills were insufficient to take notes or write my own exams, I had no trouble using my adaptive equipment to mark up textbooks or make outlines. As a result, I never fell far behind or had to burn the midnight oil to cram for a test.

I used my typewriter often. Once, I translated the entire novel used in my German reading class from German to English, one key stroke at a time. When the final test required only the translation of several large paragraphs from the novel; I was able to dictate my answer from memory. My grade point average slipped a bit from the South Dakota days, but I still made the Dean's list every semester.

As the first year at Mizzou progressed, there was one problem that needed attention. I was not happy with my helper. He was meeting my physical needs but we were increasingly incompatible. For one thing, he considered himself a cosmopolitan intellectual and me a country hick. Even worse, he could sleep through any disaster known to man. Once asleep, I couldn't wake him. On one occasion, I had planned to study for a German test for an extra hour before class but he was sleeping so soundly I couldn't roust him. I was fortunate to wake him in time to get to class.

With Jim Pelton, whose faithfulness allowed me to complete my studies.

The solution happened by sheer luck, a recurring theme in my life. I met a fellow student and dorm member, Jim Pelton. Jim is living proof that mothers aren't kidding when they tell you that running with scissors could put out an eye. He lost his right eye to a scissors at age three; that steered him towards college rather than the family water-pump and well-drilling business. Jim and I rapidly formed a partnership that was to last for the next four years. This stability allowed me to concentrate on college; it allowed Jim to pursue his education with some extra coins in his pocket. We haven't been in contact for many years now, each too busy with his chosen career, but I'll never forget Jim and his contribution to my success.

Also, in the fall of 1964, I met someone else destined to play a major role in my life for the next four decades, my buddy Irven

Friedhoff. Irv was a skinny kid from Iowa with black horn-rimmed glasses who had a bout with spinal meningitis as a young teenager that left him partially paralyzed. He walked with great difficulty using crutches. Irv and I have been best friends almost from the first moment we met in the dorm. He was the class "brainiac" in his small-town high school and was, and still is, the most avid reader I know. His vocational rehabilitation counselor thought he'd make a fine watchmaker after trade school but wiser heads insisted that Iowa pony up the money to send him to the University of Missouri. Irv soon abandoned his original plan of becoming a teacher and, like me, started aiming towards law school. Our paths have run parallel ever since.

The undergraduate years at Mizzou were among the happiest years of my life. I truly enjoyed the challenge of higher education and the opportunity to commingle with new friends. Even with my self-imposed study habits, there was plenty of time for fun. A big university is a whole community unto itself. It offers many extracurricular activities from athletics, to lectures, to concerts by popular and well-known artists. My dorm buddies and I went to many events at Brewer Fieldhouse and Jesse Hall; we were regulars at football and basketball games. In addition, there were many interesting "dives" and restaurants around the fringes of campus. My favorite was the Italian Village where we gathered regularly for a pizza and a pitcher of beer. Although we were dismounted, everything was within walking distance and I had a ready source of manpower to push my wheelchair.

Focus and commitment are the keys to success in any endeavor. If nothing else, I learned this from my own successes and watching the failures of others. Some of my dorm mates, disabled and "AB" alike, lost sight of their academic goals in the midst of all the partying and outside activities. The failure to focus on study brought the dreaded "Notice of Probation." Continued failure meant dismissal at the end of the semester.

And then there were girls. College is a wonderful time to explore the relationship between the sexes. Many romances blossomed in my dorm but as always, in the search for love, there were many disappointments as well. Those who pursued love at all costs suffered academically. Some of my handicapped friends suffered the worst. Relationships can be difficult for anyone but especially so for the disabled. When one brings physical impairments to the table, the right choices are few and finding the right one even harder. Since relationships are considered the norm, it was crushing for many who reached out and were rejected. Without much difficulty, I avoided those entanglements. For one thing, I have a great deal of adaptive equipment that prevents anybody from getting too close physically. Even more, I was exceedingly wary of developing emotional attachments. Although I wanted romance as much as anybody, the chance of success seemed remote. I decided to concentrate instead on my studies and wait for the opposite sex to approach me. Nobody did.

With all the pieces in place, my educational journey continued without further interruption. The University of Missouri was a perfect place to apply the lessons I learned about survival. I immersed myself in the courses and looked forward to the beginning of each fall semester after spending my summers at home.

12

Independence: The Challenges

The University of Missouri was my first opportunity to practice independent living. It was here that I put many strategies into practice, strategies that evolved into an independent way of life in spite of physical disabilities. The life of a paralyzed individual is very complicated under the best of circumstances; I would have been the world's happiest ditch digger had this passed me by. There's a line in a Bob Dylan song in which he laments that an ex-lover "would rather see [him] paralyzed." I can't think of a worse curse; that relationship must have ended very badly. I've often told people: "Don't ever be a cripple!" It's usually good for a laugh, but I'm deadly serious. I'm as helpless as a newborn; I have all the needs of a baby, and I'm not nearly as cute. Worse than that, I weigh a hundred and seventy-five pounds; that's one big baby.

The term "quadriplegia" refers to the condition of paralysis in all four limbs. Those afflicted with spinal injuries lose all nerve function as well. Unlike spinal injuries, a post-polio individual does not lose sensory perception; my pain and sensory nerves are very much alive. I have full bowel and bladder control. Kids often ask me how I go to the bathroom and I tell them "with help."

The first, and maybe the hardest lesson I learned about quadriplegia is that it didn't automatically make me the center of the universe. Paralysis didn't entitle me to anything. If I choose to make it so, people end up resenting it, and disliking me. This realization began during my time at St. Joe's Rehab in Omaha. I learned much by watching another patient there. He thought he was entitled to special privileges simply because he was paralyzed. He demanded and demanded, whined and complained. Nobody liked him, and more importantly, nobody went out of their way to help him. My fellow patient never learned the old saw that you have to get to know somebody before you can use and abuse them.

Family is different. Bound by blood and love, they will allow you to claim some "center of the universe" status. Usually, they will go the extra mile for you without complaint. But for everybody else, friendship only goes so far. Respect must be earned; it's a bit more complicated for the disabled because of the constant need to ask for help.

My first week on campus at the University of Missouri was the first time since becoming paralyzed that I was truly on my own. During that week I had a chance encounter with a man in a wheelchair. His name and his mission have long since been forgotten, but his words will never be: "If you want to live independently, people are the key. Engage and cultivate them constantly to help meet your needs." What a prophet! I tried faithfully to put his advice into practice, engaging people wherever and whenever I could. Many people, good friends, acquaintances, colleagues and even total strangers, have helped me out. The list of people who've stood by me with no apparent reward for their actions is mind-boggling. I would have gone nowhere in this world without them.

College was an excellent training ground. Living in a dorm, I had access to many young people in close quarters. In addition, we disabled kids looked out for each other. Lacking mobility, I was stuck in my room at times until my roommate returned. I tried to avoid being an undue burden but if a situation became truly desperate, I would yell or whistle. Eventually someone would look in on me. In dealing with these situations, I worked hard to control my temper. Other than a brief moment of self-satisfaction, anger or bitterness only makes things worse. It's better to rejoice at the end of an ordeal and move on.

As time passed, I learned the necessity of making sacrifices. This involves a keen sense of priority. What is important? What became important to me as the process evolved was getting an education, getting a job, and living the most normal life I could under the circumstances. That didn't include a lot of social occasions, or dating, or most things that people consider good times.

Lack of mobility kept me away from many gatherings. It was difficult to arrange transportation where any distance was involved, and I was very sensitive about asking people to assume my burdens. Lugging a wheelchair up or down steps is not an easy task and I was very aware of the dangers to me and my equipment. My near mishap in South Dakota was etched in my brain. Risk taking must carry with it the opportunity for reward, and self-pleasure wasn't good enough.

There were always self-imposed limitations. Public places with steps were to be avoided. I treated physical barriers as the ultimate symbol that my presence wasn't welcome. Instead of whining about it, I simply took my business elsewhere. As I developed a close circle of friends, I did have the opportunity to indulge in more social events, public and private. These were welcome forays into the world of normality. However, the same rules were in place; I needed a good reason to risk taking the stairs at a friend's house, and complete trust in my strongest friends.

Public places in America have undergone dramatic changes in the past fifty years. As a new wheelchair user, I was confronted constantly with architectural barriers from curbs to steps to narrow doors to cramped hallways. Now, barriers are becoming a thing of the past. Curb cuts have become commonplace, ramps and lifts are replacing steps; most public buildings and businesses have doors that open automatically or with the touch of a button. There are larger hallways and more accessible bathrooms as well. This has been a boon to both the disabled and the general public. I smile every time I see a young mother pushing a baby stroller over a curb cut or up a ramp, or see shoppers with both arms full walking through the automatic doors at retail stores. Mobility has gotten easier for all of us.

The most critical aspect of living independently is hiring people as personal-care attendants. I created a newspaper ad that I used to hire a helper when I needed one, which was often. Over time, my skill at picking people from the applications improved. That is to say, I learned quickly who to reject immediately. However, finding the best fit is a matter of trial and error; experience on the job is the only true test. It takes a great deal of patience to work through those first two weeks. I was often surprised by the way things developed. Some, whose strength was questionable going in, turned out to be surprisingly strong. Others, whose strength was obvious, were very rough. Some were not offended in any way by the intimate details of personal care; others were.

During my rehab days I learned how to identify my needs and how to instruct people to best meet them. In the real world, I learned an equally important lesson: identifying other people's limitations. People come with their own set of problems: social, moral, financial, whatever. Many times I watched my helpers get into really bad situations. Often, I thought I knew how to help them. In pursuit of my self-interest, I tried to convince them that they were pursuing a self-destructive course, hoping they would be grateful and more willing to stay with me. But it doesn't work that way. I soon learned the danger of getting involved in the personal problems of others. Usually, they don't listen anyway, or even thank you for your input. Often, it involved the loan of money which in most cases was never returned. Worse, many of them resented my efforts and my level of care deteriorated accordingly. Still, it's a very difficult lesson; I wish I could learn how to remain permanently detached and avoid playing God.

When something goes terribly wrong with a helper, the objective is to get them out of your life as quickly as possible. But, until there is a suitable replacement, this requires a certain level of diplomacy. A quadriplegic friend of mine had the nerve to fire a helper after he'd placed him on the toilet. He had suffered enough of the guy's impudence and told him quite forcefully to get out of the house immediately. Now there's a bold move; my friend had a lot of faith in his backup plan.

Over the years, I've had my share of incompetent, or worse, helpers as well. At least two of them ended up in jail for trying to steal from me. One broke into my firesafe while I was working and stole several of my blank checks and forged my signature. One part of me is shocked by that; the other part is amused that someone would think I had so little control over my environment that I didn't know I was being ripped off. I may be paralyzed, but I'm not stupid.

For many years, my helpers lived with me; room and board were part of the pay package. I was blessed with many good people who answered my ads; many of them are still dear friends and remain in contact. Even my cousin Jim took a turn while Uncle LeRoy was teaching at a university in Saudi Arabia. The family thought it wise that we look after each other; Jim finished high school and started college under my guardianship.

When in-home care was no longer feasible, my helper would leave after putting me to bed. It was unsettling when that front door slammed shut for the night; I had to adjust to spending the night alone. I'm told that Franklin Roosevelt, perhaps the most famous polio survivor, was terrified of fire. That's not my problem; I'm frightened by storms. Lying helplessly in bed while lightening flashes and thunder cracks above you can be very unnerving; add a warning siren blaring in the night, that's terror.

The nightly ritual requires preparation and attention to detail to insure that the night is spent in comfort. If something isn't right, the night can be very long. I deal with it as best I can. If something goes wrong, the last resort is to disturb a friend's rest. I'm a worrier by nature, which is helpful for remembering mundane details, but the added pressure of thinking ahead does little to quell anxieties. My former pulmonary doctor, Dr. Oscar Schwartz, to whom I owe a great debt for showing me how to cope with post-polio breathing difficulties, once told me: "Dick, you have to stop worrying so much." I told him: "Doc, if you're dependent on somebody to get you up in the morning and to do all your necessities for you, you're going to worry. That's my life!"

If my caregiver didn't show up in the morning, I had to deal with it by finding somebody else. I've been deserted many times; but for some reason, maybe my guardian angel, somebody always showed up to rescue me. Any attempt to recall or catalog all the times when something went wrong would be a wasted effort. Why bother? Human mistakes and failures are part of life; everybody makes them, everybody has to deal with them. When someone doesn't show up, or misplaces something I need, or fails to use the proper procedures for making me comfortable, or fails to hook the control on the wheelchair properly, or whatever, I must take responsibility for the shortcoming and bear the consequences. That's the price of independence; it's the same for everybody. In my case, the consequences can be more immediate and sometimes a bit more dramatic, that's all.

For thirty-four years I lived in the same apartment in Columbia, Missouri. It was part of a large complex; the buildings were three stories high and grouped around a large courtyard with a common passageway in front of each building. Most of the occupants were college students and because of the close proximity of the individual apartments, the place had a dorm-like atmosphere. It was a great place to collect people. Since the ultimate backup plan for dealing with any difficulty requires people, I did my best to cultivate relationships with my neighbors. I'm not a gregarious person by nature; small talk and gossip bore me quickly. However, striking up a conversation had long since ceased to be a burden or necessary evil devoted solely to self-interest. Over time, I have learned to enjoy the art of conversation; it can be both entertaining and enlightening. Moreover, for those willing to participate, it is an opportunity for me to dispel any preconceived notions of "ogre or freak." The whole experience has helped me form many deep and lasting friendships, and a few enemies.

This process kept me going when my paid helpers let me down. My working arrangement with helpers in those days allowed them to pursue their education or other interests during the day after packing me off to work during the week. Once I had a helper who seemed to think he could leave on Friday and not come back until Monday. Thank God for friends! My neighbor, Norman C. Ronald, would take over for the entire weekend. Over the years, if it wasn't Norman, it was the Orr brothers, or Joe Fink, or "Big Al" Parish, or Tim Hennessy, or Sharon Peirick, or Kevin West, or cousin Bob, or countless others. Of course the main man was my best friend, Irv Friedhoff. He lived next door for almost thirty years and, in spite of his own disabilities, always looked after me. I could count on

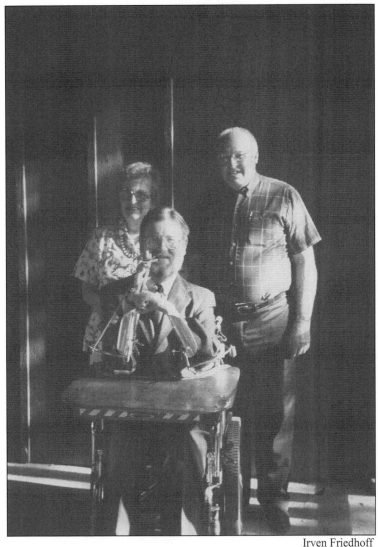

Irven Friedhoff

My Parents

Irv to find help when I needed it. Without him, I would have fallen through the cracks many times over.

The ultimate alternative was my parents. There were times when I had to call on them for weeks at a time until new arrangements could be made. This option was the last resort. Although they were always willing, I thought my independence was one fruit of their sacrifices and they should be free to live their own lives.

Finding the right people and maintaining a regular schedule are the keys to living independently. In spite of my best efforts, two parts of the body do not respond well to schedules or time tables: the bladder and the bowel. As a polio survivor, I have sensation and control over these bodily functions; as a quadriplegic, I can't do anything for myself when nature calls. This leads to interesting dilemmas when pursuing an independent life. As usual, it's people to the rescue. My colleagues accepted my condition and I maintained a list of ready volunteers for bladder calls. However, there are times when nobody is available; dark clothing helps.

The bowel is another matter. To a disabled person, diarrhea is a scourge. It is embarrassing, frustrating, humiliating, dehumanizing, and also smelly. At times it strikes for no apparent reason other than nerves. One of my helpers, Al Parish, dubbed my attacks *"homo eruptus."* On one memorable occasion, diarrhea struck during a visit with Uncle LeRoy and family. We were returning to central Washington after a sightseeing trip to Seattle when I screamed, "Uncle, find a bathroom quickly!" We were traveling on a busy Interstate in the city, good luck! About a minute later, I called out, "Never mind."

We decided the best option was to make the three-hour trip back to his house and deal with the situation there. Upon arrival, my cousin Lisa, who was sitting closest to me during the trip, vanished in search of fresh air. LeRoy, Joanie, and Cousin Jim began the task of cleanup immediately. The best option was to lower me to the linoleum floor outside the bathroom and start peeling away the layers of soiled clothing. Joanie was cutting off my T-shirt with scissors because it was too messy to pull over my head when Uncle nonchalantly remarked, "Wouldn't it be easier to drag him to the backyard and turn the hose on him?"

Humor is part of the genetic code of my family. It percolates under the surface, ready to pop out at any moment. It's the greatest coping agent I know for dealing with life's darker moments. By the time the laughter and the giggles subsided, the task was done. Clothing can be washed, bodies can be cleaned; life goes on.

In the college of life, I have attained advanced degrees in efficiency and time management. Both are essential to accomplish more than just maintenance in the daily life of someone with severe disabilities. By reducing everyday tasks to the simplest routines, and by budgeting my time, I became a full-time student and later a full-time employee.

13

Law School

Having spent the summer at home, I returned to campus in the fall of 1964 eager to resume on-the-job training in living independently. The folks dropped me off at the dorm and I introduced them to my friend and new caregiver, Jim Pelton. As mentioned previously, Jim's contributions during these formative years can not be overstated. After settling in, the first task was touring the hall, greeting friends and meeting the new faces. It was also the opportunity to compare schedules to see who was available to push me to and from classes where necessary. That didn't take long; my friends were there for me.

I was enrolled in the College of Arts and Science, but the idea of law school was still planted firmly in my mind. I made several inquiries about the requirements for admission. I was told that the University of Missouri School of Law would accept undergraduates if they had scored well on the Law School Admission Test and completed all of the prerequisites for their bachelor's degree by the end of their junior year. In such case, the first thirty hours of law school could be added to the accumulated undergraduate credit hours needed for a bachelor's degree. In short, my senior year in college could be spent as a first-year law student. This was perfect. I could get back one of those lost years in my educational journey.

I was pursuing a BA with a major in History and a minor in Political Science. I completed and filed the necessary "Area of Concentration" forms with my academic advisor, outlining a plan to finish all required courses for obtaining a BA by the end of my junior year. My plan barely met the minimum requisites for a BA and left no room for "fun" elective courses. But it was doable by carrying the normal fifteen credit hours per semester, as long as I didn't fail any course.

Things proceeded according to the plan and I made the necessary arrangements to take the LSAT in the spring of 1965. If there were special materials to read, or a study course for preparation, I was unaware of them. I prepared by drinking a few beers with my dorm buddies at a local pub the night before, and then off early to bed. The test itself was unlike anything I'd taken before. Most of it is now a blur but I do recall many multiple choice questions asking to pick a symbol closest to the ones set forth in the question. At first glance the symbols had nothing in common; it took some thinking to decipher the common thread.

There were three categories to the test: law aptitude, general knowledge, and English. I was disappointed with my English score, 57th percentile, but I scored in the 75th percentile on general knowledge and over the 90th percentile on law aptitude. Armed with that score and a GPA hovering around 3.5, I filed my application to the University of Missouri School of Law. I wasn't surprised when my application was accepted; I thought my credentials were very good.

Many years went by before I discovered how narrow the margin of victory had been. I learned it through a colleague who shared an office with me for a time. She had married the dean of the law school, Joe Covington, some years after I graduated. During one of our many conversations she told me how proud her husband was of my success and how I had more than justified his decision to press for my admittance into law school.

"What do you mean," said I; "I posted very good credentials for admission." It was then I was told that my grades and test score weren't the determining factor initially. The regular admission committee had rejected my application. They were convinced that my physical condition would preclude success in law school; I wouldn't be able to carry the full load necessary to complete the program in the allotted three years. Luckily for me, the matter was forwarded for faculty review and further consideration. Dean Covington carried the day at the faculty review process. With support from two other faculty members, he argued that my success to date and the good LSAT score dictated a positive response. He said I deserved the opportunity to join the incoming class. Angels are everywhere, even in law school.

When the class of 1968 assembled in Tate Hall for orientation in the fall of 1965, it was the largest class assembled to that time, over one hundred and fifty strong with one lonely wheelchair user and two women. As usual, I was a minority of one. After a welcoming speech which included the usual tributes to the high academic standards of our class, we were given a glimpse of the challenge ahead. One of my assumptions was quickly dashed. Our credentials didn't guarantee a place at the graduation ceremonies. Instead of fighting to keep us, the professors seemed determined to throw us out. We were solemnly informed that the first year of law school would be a "weeding out" process. The faculty fully expected to lose half of the class by year's end. The Dean put it to us bluntly: "I want you to look at the person on your right and then the person on your left. It is likely that one of them will no longer be here next year."

My new classmates were much different than the guys in the dorm. Most of them were already graduates, many were married, and some had had several years of work experience before returning to school. One thing most seemed to have in common was a professional family background. I met many whose fathers and grandfathers were lawyers and who had probably grown up listening to legal issues being discussed at the dinner table. When asked where my father practiced law, I just laughed and said, "Dad fattens cattle and raises pigs." Add that to my appearance and I must have been considered quite the oddity; I suspect the betting was against my being there the next year. However, I wasn't prepared to admit that my background would limit success in law school, or the legal profession. Some values like hard work, sacrifice, and honesty, are universal. In addition, my upbringing and experiences taught me things they'd never know. Heritage doesn't guarantee success in law school, I reasoned. Bravado covers a multitude of uncertainties but, even so, I was beginning to have some doubts about this law school thing.

The doubts were swept away temporarily by the rigorous class schedule. Tate Hall was barely adequate to handle the crowd. The hallways were packed between classes as three grades of law students jostled to the next class. I didn't lack for volunteers to push me through the mob; at least I didn't have to be pushed from building to building. Every course in the first year was required. The stated aim of the law school was to prepare each student for the Missouri Bar Exam, the final hurdle before one could be licensed to practice law. The law school prided itself on the fact that few students flunked the exam. Maintaining that standard was the task of the biggest collection of eccentric professors I could ever imagine. A classmate whose father graduated from law school said that the three year experience could best be summed up this way: "In the first year, they scare the hell out of you; in the second year, they work the hell out of you; in the third year, they bore the hell out of you."

The first part of the triangle was certainly proving true. The teaching method could best be described as old-fashioned, maybe medieval. It had only been a year or so that the requirement of wearing a coat and tie to each class and standing to recite had been dropped. We were subjected to a never ending barrage of case-law study in such courses as contracts, torts, property law, criminal law, and civil procedure. This meant studying legal decisions every day for discussion in class. If you were unprepared and unlucky enough to be called upon, you were summarily tossed out of that class for the day. It was mental boot camp at its finest with drill instructors that would have made the Marine Corps proud. Even with preparation, a student was often left flustered and frustrated by the sharp questioning which followed his initial presentation. Our professors were experts in their field and well-schooled in the art of springing the trap on the unwary. Many were the victims who assumed they had mastered the details of a case, only to be destroyed by withering cross-examination. I was actually relieved that I couldn't raise my hand in class. My new motto became "Prepare carefully, listen intently, and stay low."

The faculty had several memorable professors of long standing tenure. Tales of their exploits were passed down from generation to generation of law students; many were true. With nicknames like "The Fox," and "The Rabbit," they inspired fear in the hearts of first-year students. "The Fox" was a slender, almost gaunt, old man with snow white hair and moustache, always impeccably dressed in a dark suit and tie. He taught Contracts but, even more, he taught us humility about our past accomplishments. The Fox made it clear that the law required more analysis than anything we had done elsewhere. "The Rabbit" taught the course in property law. He was a portly individual, florid of face, with a slight speech impediment. His "r" was pronounced like a "w." The Rabbit didn't suffer fools gladly and his roar of disapproval was withering. While the Fox destroyed presentations with swift and witty rapier thrusts, the Rabbit preferred the blunt force of a battle axe.

We were expected to be at our desks with book open when the professor arrived to start class. The Fox did not tolerate students being late to his class. He locked the door upon entry and ignored any knocking that ensued subsequently. He told the students sitting near the door: "Do not open that door." One day a student walking down the hall to class noticed the Fox approaching behind him. He paused at the door to allow him to enter first; the Fox did and shut the door in his face, locking it. The student was left standing in the hallway.

Whatever the underlying reason for this approach to legal education, it certainly was an effective way of cutting the class size. Those whose fathers had been subjected to this treatment may have had a distinct advantage; the rest of us were simply intimidated.

The next stage of our transition from normal human beings to law students was the famous "trial exam." We had been told at orientation that exams were only given once at the end of each term, a four-hour exam for each course. Supposedly, the trial exam was designed to simulate a real law school exam. We had been advised to form our own study groups to prepare for exams. Somehow the various cliques that formed broke into study groups. I managed to attach myself to a group of people I thought were serious students, but over time decided the group was too large to be manageable. I needed access to their notes but had serious misgivings about the various methods of case-law analysis. I thought it best to seek the core finding first, the heart of the decision, and then work outwards to the subsidiary findings. For many in the group, the approach was to start at the periphery and work inward with plenty of pontification along the way. By semester's end, my group was down to two. Hugh McPheeters had become my study partner and we worked well together throughout law school.

The trial exam was scheduled for an evening in October. It was my first opportunity to use the equipment supplied by the school to take my exams. The faculty would not consider oral testing or my previous method of dictating to a helper. Instead, the Dean proposed a dictation machine with foot controls, the same controls used by the secretaries. With a little practice, I found I could control the on and off function with my left foot. That was it. I had to dictate my answers to a machine with little opportunity to revise or extend them. The tape was transcribed by the Dean's secretary and then given to the professor for grading. I was not allowed to review the typed product. Numbers were assigned to each paper instead of names. Supposedly this kept the professor from knowing whose paper he was grading. None of us believed that.

Exams in law school were taken on the honor system; students spread out over the building looking for a quiet spot to write or type their exams. I was assigned a small cubicle in the bowels of the library. My caregiver helped set up the machine and spread my trial exam over my lapboard before exiting. The trial exam involved contracts and that meant our grader would be the Fox. As best I remember, the exam was scheduled for two hours. About an hour in, the building shook slightly. "Did you feel that?" was a common question as we gathered in small knots afterwards. A passing upper classman said it was probably caused by the collective knee shaking of the first-year students. Actually, it was a small tremor caused by a slight shift in the New Madrid Fault in Southeast Missouri. For the superstitious it was definitely an omen.

"The trial exam grades are in." That phrase echoed through the halls as we arrived for classes. The noise quickly turned to silence as we examined our papers. The criticisms on the papers were terse; it seems we had learned nothing about the law of contracts. The grade on my paper said "F" with several minus signs behind it. One student had seventeen minus signs behind his "F." Rumor had it that another didn't get a grade, just a dime taped to his exam with a note that said: "Call your mother and tell her you won't be a lawyer." To the enlightened among us this was simply another phase in the transition process. It was a practice exam they said, the grade didn't even count; there was no reason for alarm. Not so for me. I was used to being considered a good student, someone near the top of the heap. This sign of failure was terrifying.

With finals looming I scheduled an appointment with the Dean of Arts and Science. "I'd like to drop out of law school, finish my undergraduate hours, and go to graduate school in History," I told the Dean. He was very understanding but told me that it was too late to drop now; I'd have to wait until the next year to reenter Arts and Science. He suggested I finish the first year of law school and use those hours to get my BA. If I was still unhappy, I could apply for grad school. The thought of wasting another year didn't appeal to me. I returned to my law books determined to finish the first year, however it turned out.

As finals approached, the normal banter and bustle around Tate Hall ceased; we all turned to our notes and books full of scribbled margins with a grim resolve to prove our worth. A smug third-year student told me that the grades from our first finals were the most critical. He explained it this way: "Your first grades place you on one of three wheels, the gold wheel, the silver wheel, or the excrement wheel. Once you're placed on one of those wheels, you're likely to stay there throughout law school, assuming you make it. The gold wheel is the top ten percent, those who will be awarded the Order of the Coif, law school's highest honor. The next 15 percent or less land on the silver wheel; the rest are stuck on the excrement wheel."

I landed on the silver wheel. When the grades were posted, I found myself in the 12th position. I had survived the crucible and come out much better than I thought I would. The four-hour exams had been complex, I left each one without a good feeling, but the proof that I belonged was posted on the board. I accepted the congratulations of my comrades with a mixture of satisfaction and relief.

The biggest disappointment was the "C" I got in Contracts I. The Fox had given us six questions to be answered in four hours. I allotted forty minutes to each answer, determined to address every issue. Leaving the exam, I bumped into another student. "That was tough, Dick," he said. "I only got through four questions; there was so much to say." I was flabbergasted to discover that he got an "A" in the course. It was rumored that the Fox only graded the first three questions. I wanted to confront him about that but lacked the courage; I've always had difficulty confronting authority figures. Their ability to help you is far outweighed by their power to destroy, or so I thought. I decided it was better to accept my grade and work harder the next time. Maybe I did, or maybe the Fox noticed my class standing; the next grade from him was much better.

The second semester was less memorable; I knew I could handle the workload. All thoughts of graduate school in History were a thing of the past. The experience in that first year changed me in so many ways. I was more analytical in my approach to problems, less assuming, better at critical thinking, less emotionally attached to issues, and in some ways more cynical. Looking back, some of the teaching techniques seemed cruel for sure, but maybe they were necessary to achieve the desired result. Somehow, I don't think so; it was not an experience I'd care to repeat.

We were given the opportunity to taste one aspect of legal practice in the second semester, something called "moot court." Moot court was an appellate proceeding in which we were required to prepare a legal brief setting forth our position and give an oral argument in support before a judicial panel. An appellate proceeding is simply a review of a trial court decision by a higher court. My opponent was a good classmate, John Z. Williams. We each got a copy of the transcript of the proceedings at the trial level, and prepared our written statements accordingly. After oral arguments before the panel, our performance was evaluated and we were given advice for improvement. I lost. The panel said I had done a good job overall but thought I had missed a question of jurisdiction. That is, they wanted me to discuss the legal issue of whether they had the authority to even hear such a case on appeal. It was a lesson in critical thinking that came without penalty, other than losing a hypothetical case to a good guy.

Other things of significance were happening that spring. On the down side, I spent spring break in the University hospital with a kidney stone. The pain was intense, but I consoled myself with the knowledge that it wasn't costing me class time.

On the positive side, Dad had scraped together enough money to buy a graduation present, a new van. With numerous modifications, it eliminated the need for transfers to and from my wheelchair and in turn gave me new freedom. We named it the "War Wagon" because of its odd appearance. With the "War Wagon," it was possible to leave the communal life of my undergraduate years. The time had come to abandon Defoe Hall, my dorm home for three years. As the second year of law school began, I was living in an apartment several miles from campus with Jim Pelton, my long standing caregiver, and two other able-bodied friends from the dorm. With three drivers, I had all the flexibility necessary to get back and forth from classes. My diploma arrived in the mail during the month of August. It was now official; I was a graduate of the University of Missouri with a BA in History. It meant nothing to me at the time; I refused to participate in graduation ceremonies.

The second year was exactly as predicted; the faculty worked the hell out of us. The courses seemed designed to flood us with a wealth of information without the prior scare tactics. In addition to the regular class assignments, I had a few extracurricular responsibilities. The law school published a Law Review quarterly, a publication devoted to legal articles and reviews of recent cases. As a member of the Dean's List, I was invited to join the Review and submit articles for publication. Over the next two years, I submitted four case notes for consideration.

The frenzy to avoid being "weeded out" was gone. The sense of competition was more lighthearted; we joked with each other as only survivors can. One course that year was taught in the trial practice courtroom, the only room in Tate Hall that was not accessible at the time. There was no way to get a wheelchair to the courtroom floor. It was a source of merriment for the class and professor alike to see me perched alone at the top of the stairs while they were huddled below. Somebody jokingly dubbed me "the class vulture." I was just happy there was a level spot inside of the doors to park my wheelchair. If nothing else, this convinced me not to sign up for the course called Trial Practice. I had no idea what I would do with my law degree, but I figured I could learn how to conduct a trial on my own if it was necessary. Assuming, that is, the courtroom didn't have steps.

One sure sign of the fact that I had been fully accepted by my class was the number of times I was the target of jokes. When the final exam for the course in the trial courtroom was handed out, I was sitting outside waiting for my helper to collect my copy. As one of the students passed by, paper in hand, I called out: "Hey, Jack, push the elevator button for me; I'd like the elevator here when Jim comes back with my exam." He glanced up from his copy and said, "It's exam time, Wieler, every man for himself," and he kept on walking. I was still laughing when Jim got there with my exam. I don't think he saw the humor in it.

My light mood vanished twenty minutes later. As I was getting ready to dictate my answer to the first question, my foot slipped off of the on-off pedal. Jim was allowed to check on me every hour; so my only recourse was to wait. I tried to stay calm as I read the entire exam and mentally prepared my answers. Thankfully, Jim returned on time and the delay didn't prevent me from getting my answers on the tape. It took some fast talking though.

Thanks to the van and my new mobility, I got a summer job at the end of the second year. Dr. Lester Wolcott, the head of the Department of Physical Medicine and Rehabilitation at the

University of Missouri Medical School, asked me to stay in town for the summer and do some research on the various laws dealing with disability. Jim Pelton and some of the other roommates had summer jobs too so it worked out perfectly. I had met Dr. Wolcott several years earlier when his department fitted me with a new corset. He was the most outgoing and optimistic doctor I met on that staff. For $300 per month, I researched the laws relating to disability. In three months I produced a position paper for Dr. Wolcott titled "Disability and the Law." He had it published in some medical journal and invited me to speak at several seminars. There wasn't a great body of work on the topic at the time and the doctors at those seminars seemed eager for my input.

Armed with an extra $900, the first money I had earned since age 15, I was ready for the final year of law school. My best friend Irv had been accepted into the incoming first-year class and joined us in renting an old house with plenty of space. We added another roommate as well so there were now four able-bodied friends to help with chores. I used some of my money to buy lumber for a ramp. The guys built a fantastic ramp to the back porch with the lumber; it was admired by everybody in the neighborhood.

I'm not sure I accept the stated prophesy that the third year of law school is boring. The work load seemed lighter but by then we knew what was expected of us. However, things were winding down and most of my classmates were actively seeking employment. The school scheduled several job fairs in the spring of 1968 where law firms throughout the region could interview upcoming graduates. I didn't sign up for any interviews. I was still focused on my courses, trying mightily to move to that gold wheel. It wasn't to be, I stayed near the top of the silver wheel, finally graduating number 13 out of a total of 108. The Order of the Coif escaped me.

One day near the end of the final semester, I was summoned to the office of Professor Elwood Thomas, our Tax and Corporations instructor. "Dick," he said; "you haven't signed up for any interviews. What are your plans after graduation?" I confessed I didn't have any. My journey to date had been accomplished one step at a time; thinking too far ahead had never been productive. It was too much like daydreaming. I told him of my concern that most firms wouldn't hire someone in a wheelchair. He agreed and said my best opportunity for employment was with government. With that in mind, he had arranged an interview with the Missouri Attorney General's Office.

Norman Anderson was the sitting Attorney General; my interview was conducted by his first assistant, Tom Downey. At the conclusion, I was offered a job as an assistant attorney general with a starting salary of $600 a month plus medical benefits, contingent upon passing the Missouri Bar Exam.

I had difficulty holding back the tears when thanking Professor Thomas for his help. It was a dream come true I told him. In spite of all my academic progress, I had doubts, sometimes big doubts, about holding a job in my condition. The opportunity to do so had just been handed to me. The only remaining barrier was the Bar Exam. I started preparing as soon as finals were over.

Courtesy of the University of Missouri School of Law

Law School Class of 1968: that's me on the corner.

I told the Dean's office that I was skipping the graduation ceremonies. Dean Covington called shortly thereafter asking me to reconsider. I wish now that I had. It never occurred to me that my professors and classmates were also proud of my achievements and wanted a chance collectively to say so. My personal concerns denied them and my family the occasion to applaud. Success earned is best shared with those who had something to do with it, and even those who didn't. At the time, I wasn't ready to admit or accept success; there were more things to do.

14

Adaptations

The five years at the University of Missouri were a valuable testing ground for my adaptive devices. Without specialized equipment, adaptations and improvisations, my journey to independence would have been very short. Actually, the trip would have been impossible. Several of the topics and devices covered in this chapter are mentioned elsewhere, sometimes at length, because they are so vital to my story.

Topping the list are the arm devices (feeders) created for me at Warm Springs. With minimal assistance, I was able to feed myself at the dorm cafeteria and elsewhere. In spite of chance encounters with doors, walls, or people, the feeders proved to be tough and reliable. Family and friends soon learned how and where to bend or twist them to maintain the proper balance. Several outpatient visits to Warm Springs during this period kept them in good repair.

The mouthstick is an essential tool. It is my constant companion for reading, and it became a communication tool when I got an electric typewriter. It took little force to activate the keys and I could "hunt and peck" at will. It is also vital for writing; I use it to guide the right feeder with a pen attached. The Warm Springs model, molded out of dental plastic to fit my teeth, was comfortable to use but subject to breakage because the wooden dowel had to be slim to fit into the mouthpiece, and the mouthpiece itself was somewhat fragile. I broke several mouthpieces and wooden dowels pushing heavy books around in law school. I kept a supply of spares with me at all times.

That problem was solved finally by my dentist after I began working. He created a mouthpiece using dental plastic around a strong metal frame; I replaced the wooden dowel with an aluminum arrow shaft. My mouthstick is now both lightweight and sturdy; it stands up to constant use with little maintenance. As long as I don't drop it, I have easy access to the phone, thanks to the invention of the speakerphone, and to the computer. I was born too soon; I can only imagine the effect of the computer on college life.

Another important piece of equipment is my lapboard. It is my personal table, the platform from which I eat, read and write. After I was able to sit upright and use my feeders, the occupational therapists at Warm Springs provided one. However, I was encouraged to use a normal table whenever I could. I guess the theory was to look as normal as possible. This wasn't for me; I don't like being pushed up to a table. They're never in the right place or at the right height. I like my lapboard. I'm still using the one made for me by my dad's cousin Bernard over forty years ago. It has a small drawer beneath the front edge to store personal items like my billfold and my keys. It works beautifully as long as I remember to tell people not to open the drawer swiftly. There's no stop and it's possible to spill the contents all over the place.

Carrying books and materials around was another issue that needed resolution. As the list of textbooks grew, especially in law school, it was no longer possible to pile them on the lapboard. Grandma John bought a briefcase for that purpose; we fashioned loops from electrical wire and hooked it to the back of my wheelchair. Over the years, it suffered from much wear and tear and I threw more and more duct tape on it. It was truly dilapidated, and the subject of much ridicule, before I finally threw it away. I found a replacement in a wheelchair catalogue on the Internet; there are all sorts of bags specifically designed to hang on the back of a wheelchair now.

Time and again, we looked for practical ways to deal with specific problems. After knocking three of my favorite glasses off the lapboard, I started looking for ways to keep glasses from sliding around. The solution was the sand bottom cup holders that truckers use. I don't know if other disabled people had the same experiences, or if it was because I grew up in an isolated farm community, but my parents and I improvised as we went along; we had no choice.

In the mid-fifties, there seemed to be little in the way of technology or even practical advice to help disabled people get out and about. Confined to a manual wheelchair, I guess it was assumed that I would stay home. Mom says we never left the farm for a year after my return from Warm Springs. To go anywhere, my folks had to dismantle my feeders, transfer me from the chair to the car, fold and store the chair in the trunk, and reverse the process once we got to our destination. It was much easier to stay home. However, staying at home was not an option; we struggled as best we could to meet the mobility challenges throughout most of my college years. The greatest leap in mobility occurred after my first year of law school. Dad bought me a van. Unlike our prior experiences with a worn out van in South Dakota, this one was fresh from the factory. It wasn't a deluxe model; it was all Dad could afford. My new van was a small delivery truck with a ninety-inch wheel base, thirteen-inch tires, and a three-speed manual transmission mounted on the steering column. It had no side windows, no paneling, no carpet, no air conditioning, and only two front seats that sat on each side of the motor compartment. It was beautiful! It was the freedom I needed to move about without being tossed in and out of a car.

Lack of headroom was one problem that confronted us. Sitting in the wheelchair, my head rubbed the roof. Dad hired a body shop to cut a four-foot-square hole in the roof and mount a metal turret in its place to fix the problem. From the outside it looked like a big square box sitting on the top. Because of its appearance we dubbed it the "War Wagon" after a John Wayne movie of the same name. To enter the van, Dad found someone to build a two-track ramp that folded three times. Unfolded, each track was nine foot long and bolted to the floor inside the back doors. It wasn't difficult to push me up the ramp but I had to duck to get inside.

Another challenge was the need to tie the wheelchair in place. We experimented with rubber cargo straps designed to hold tarps in place on truck boxes but the problem was getting the chair into the proper position because the straps weren't that flexible. Finally, we decided to bolt seatbelts into the floor to secure the chair in place. Once in place, and tied down, I had plenty of headroom but limited visibility; we added a small window on each side to help with that. I learned the hard way about the need for seatbelts. I was on the way to get a haircut when someone cut us off and my driver slammed on the brakes

The War Wagon: the makeshift box on top gave me the headroom I needed.

to avoid a collision. I got thrown from my chair and smashed into the motor compartment between the front seats. My right knee took the brunt of the impact but nothing was broken. I did tear a ligament; it took more than a week for the swelling to go down. A friend of mine made a crude safety harness for me so it wouldn't happen again.

This ugly little duckling of a truck, powder blue in color, was the best gift ever. Knowing the sacrifice he made, it was a tangible reminder of my father's love. In the years following my experiences with the "War Wagon," an industry has grown to meet the demand for usable vehicles by the disabled. Now there are tested industry standards in place instead of our trial-and-error methods. My current vehicle is a marvel of modern engineering. The floor has been lowered for more headroom, without disturbing the overall look or design. There is a push-button operated lift on the side, instead of crude, finger-pinching

Dad loading one of his homemade ramps. My colleagues will cringe at the sight of them.

ramps. There are specifically designed tie-downs that securely hold me and the wheelchair in place. Unfortunately, all of these improvements come with a big price tag; the cost of progress is steep.

The greatest need for mobility involved wheelchairs themselves. During my entire college career, I needed assistance to push my manual chair from place to place. I was stuck in place until someone moved me. The invention of a practical motorized wheelchair was a fantastic technological advancement. However, the first guidance systems for those chairs were designed for use by those with arm and hand function. Those with none, like me, need not apply. The vision that finally put me in a motorized wheelchair began at the University of Missouri. My savior was an engineering professor and a master of adaptation. I'll deal with that at length in another chapter.

With each passing decade after my years at Mizzou, more goods and services designed specifically for the disabled became available. As they came to market the need for improvisation became less and less. For years, I slept on a hospital bed, an old-fashioned one with a metal headboard, twin-size in width. Every time I got rolled over, I skinned my elbow on the wall, or risked falling out. I needed a bigger bed, but one equipped to raise my head and knees. The only solution at the time was to widen my bed by cutting it in half and welding three-foot spacers in between. I found a body shop to do the work. Instead of springs, the base of this wider bed would have to be plywood. A local mattress factory assured me that they could make a mattress that was both flexible and comfortable. It was a firm mattress but I enjoyed the extra space.

Today, there is a market for specialty beds. They are expensive but more comfortable than my homemade contraption ever was. Currently, I own a wide bed with a mattress designed to ease the danger of developing bed sores. Bed sores were a worry during the early years but I toughened up considerably as I became more active. I don't get sore on this bed but traveling is another problem. On the rare occasions I'm away from home, the accommodations are never as comfortable. There's no place like home.

I spend more time in comfort and safety today, especially at night, because I bought an environmental control unit (ECU) in 1992. This system gives me control over many things while lying in bed. It's compact and easy to use, another by-product of the space age. With the ECU, I control the telephone, the television, and any other devices that can be operated with an off/on switch. Mounted to my bed are two pieces of the unit, a display module and a sip-and-puff tube. Sitting on a table next to the bed is the base unit with wires running to the bed, a television remote control, and the display module. By sipping or puffing on the tube I can activate any preprogrammed device. At the moment, I have control over five appliances: an electric blanket, a lamp, a fan, my stereo, and a television. I can also activate motors on the bed to raise or lower the head and knees, or the bed itself. This allows me to seek a more comfortable position should something ache, and to position the bed for easy transfer to the wheelchair.

Unfortunately, what technology gives, it can also take away. Many new household appliances are engineered to shut down when the electricity is cut off and can be restarted only by pushing the on/off button on the appliance itself. I'm still forced to adapt by seeking older but functional appliances that can be turned on and off with my system.

The world of assistive technology will only get better with time. As computers get more powerful, more functions can be assigned to them. Voice-recognition software is still in its infancy; it will be the next leap forward for me. However, there are limits to everything. Once I find something that works well for me, I am extremely reluctant to change. Friends chide me often about some of my methods and my aged and battered mechanical devices. They don't understand the chasm that exists between the many things that don't work and the few that do in the life of a cripple. I learned a long time ago not to frustrate myself needlessly over "new and improved" things. No machine can make a quadriplegic individual self-sufficient; only the most dedicated misanthrope would even want to live that way. I like people and, more importantly, I need them.

15

The Bar Exam

My time at the University of Missouri had come to an end. Against all odds, I had successfully completed college and law school. As the summer of 1968 approached, my future was starting to take shape. A job was waiting in the wings. The last remaining obstacle was the Missouri Bar Exam. My faithful caregiver for the past four years, Jim Pelton, agreed to stay on during the review period.

Reviews were held regularly at the law school during the month of June. The adversarial nature of the student-professor relationship was gone. Our professors laid out the basics of their specialties, each in turn highlighting areas that were sure to be covered on the bar exam. We were given a cram course in the various aspects of law without the question-and-answer cross-examinations.

In addition, I reviewed my notes and the course books on a daily basis. My notes consisted of materials I had borrowed from others plus the notes I had taken in class myself. My confidence at writing down the pertinent points during lectures without falling behind had finally emerged during the second year of law school. Although writing in my unique style was too slow for four-hour exams, it was adequate for taking notes. The training proved invaluable later as I made notes from court opinions for use in writing briefs or legal arguments on the job.

The Missouri Bar Exam was scheduled for mid-July. It consisted of essay questions covering the basic areas of law. The exam was conducted under the supervision of the Missouri Supreme Court in five sessions spread out over two and a half days. I had notified the Clerk of the Court about my physical limitations and the need to make special arrangements for taking the exam. The agreed on solution was for me to dictate my answers to one of the court's secretaries. By this time, I was comfortable with any method; this one was fine with me.

As the month of June came to a close, I had to say goodbye to my faithful caregiver. It was a great loss; Jim had contributed to my success in so many ways. However, it was time for him to pursue his interests. During our years together, Jim had completed college and wrapped up a master's degree in library science.

Dad was my caregiver during the three days of examination. Mom was left in charge of chores on the farm. She had become a very capable farmhand as she and Dad struggled to stay afloat. Even though the farm was in good hands, it was a sacrifice for Dad to take me to Jefferson City, Missouri, for the three-day event. After suffering terrible losses in the cattle market during the '50s, Dad had turned to raising pigs as his primary profit source. The business of raising pigs is labor-intensive. My brother was no longer available to help with chores. He had joined the Marine Corps after graduating from high school in 1967 and was stationed in California. Mom often joked that she spent more time in the pig barn than in the house.

We checked into the motel and I immediately began reviewing my notes for the next day's exam. I was scheduled to take my exams in the Supreme Court Building, a stately red-brick edifice that was home to both the Missouri Supreme Court and my future employer, the Missouri Attorney General. To our surprise, the building was not accessible. A full flight of steps blocked the front entrance so we made our approach from the rear. Only four steps barred our access to the elevator there. With a little help from the janitor, Dad negotiated the steps and deposited me with my transcriber.

It was my first opportunity to work directly with a professional secretary. I was surprised by her typing skills and the ease with which we worked together. The first session went well, the afternoon session even better. The first day was behind me. The law school professors had prepared us well; I wasn't surprised by any of the questions.

If Dad was bored in this alien environment, he never complained. I was too absorbed with my ordeal to ask him what he did while I was dictating my answers to various questions of law. The second day was more of the same, a four-hour morning session and another four-hour session after lunch. By the third day, I was ready to go home. The last morning session had some tricky questions. The secretary complimented me on one of the answers. I told her I was glad she liked it; I didn't have the slightest idea what I was talking about.

It was finally over! I had come a long way from those dreadful days of despair in 1955; the impossible dream of becoming a lawyer, hatched during my stay in the rehabilitation unit at St. Joseph's, was nearing reality. I felt totally confident as we returned to Nebraska to await the outcome. The results of the bar exam would be posted in a mere six weeks. That gave me six weeks to prepare for my first professional job. Using my contacts in the law school and the attorney general's office, I began the task of finding a place to live in Jefferson City and, more importantly, competent caregivers. From long distance, I made inquiries with those in charge of student employment at Lincoln University in Jefferson City. Lincoln is a small school with a proud black heritage; it was founded during the Civil War by black officers of the Union army stationed in Missouri's capital city. With the end of segregation, it was becoming more of a small commuter school serving the region. Most of the white students commuted daily; many of the black students lived in dorms on campus.

Two applicants offered me a unique opportunity, twin brothers from St. Louis studying at Lincoln. They were looking for a way to live off campus and agreed to take the job for room and board. With that important issue resolved, the next task was finding an accessible place to live. Jefferson City is located in the middle of the state and laid out along the south bank of the Missouri River. Like most river towns, it is hilly in nature and most buildings are fronted by steps. With some searching, we found a ground level apartment with no barriers that was acceptable to me and the twins. The stage was now set.

The results of the bar exams were posted in early September. As I expected, I passed. A friend of mine used to brag that he got one of the highest grades ever given on the bar exam. Since the exam is graded either "pass" or "fail," I guess I did too. The swearing-in ceremony to the Missouri Bar was scheduled for the following Saturday. This time Mom joined Dad to watch me being sworn in along with my classmates and students from other schools. Dad found somebody to do chores on the farm so they could both get away. The ceremony was conducted by the chief judge of the court in a courtroom, one of two, in the Missouri Supreme Court Building. At that moment, I could never have imagined how many times I would appear in that courtroom in the years to come.

This time, I was just in awe at the magnitude of the moment. As we broke into little groups after the ceremony, my parents finally got the opportunity to meet my classmates and some of the professors. Mom was especially impressed by her chat with Dean Covington.

"That man is so proud of your accomplishments," she said.

"They would have been better if he had given me a better grade in one of his classes," I grumbled. At that point, I wasn't ready to concede that law professors possessed normal human emotions. She just shook her head and gave me that look that only mothers can when their child says something stupid. Mom was so right of course, as I discovered much later.

16

Transition

The time for ceremony was over; it was time to go to work. My meager belongings were in place, my wardrobe, such as it was, was clean and ready, and the twins were trained and settled into their quarters. It had been a painful experience watching them learn to drive with a manual transmission on the hilly streets of Jefferson City. Thankfully, the War Wagon survived the ordeal. We had made the necessary arrangements for help negotiating the four steps into the rear of the Supreme Court Building. The folks had hurried back to their chores after the weekend ceremonies. On Monday, the twins dropped me off and headed to their classes.

Safely inside, I was wheeled about the office and introduced to the staff. My new secretary was a young woman fresh out of secretarial school and only a year into the job. "Mary Ann, we'll have to learn how to do this together; I'll need your help," I told her.

The office itself was laid out on two floors. The upper floor was the main entrance from the lofty front of the building. It had

Pamela Norman Shoup

Working in the office.

high ceilings with ornate pillars at regular intervals. My office was on the lower floor with low ceilings and overhead pipes.

Most of the offices were cramped and occupied by two people. Things always look different on the inside.

I signed the necessary paperwork, took the oath of office as an assistant attorney general, and was escorted to my desk. My first task was already waiting. The transcript and the legal briefs for both sides in an appellate criminal case were laid out for me. I was scheduled to appear before the Missouri Supreme Court the next morning to argue the state's position. In Missouri, and probably in many other states, criminal cases are handled by local prosecutors at the trial level, but all appeals from convictions are handled by the attorney general. This was truly baptism under fire; I was to appear before the court only three days after being sworn in. Later, I discovered this was normal procedure for the attorney general's office. Young lawyers were put in harness immediately.

Somehow I survived my first court appearance and the first week of work, and then the second. Things got easier and easier as my routine in the office and at home became established. Within months, a wooden ramp was built to a new door at the rear of the building. Someone had taken note of my daily battle with the four steps. Much later, a permanent concrete ramp was built on the inside of the back door.

The local circuit court was not equipped with a ramp, however, and my first foray there proved memorable. The entry with the fewest steps was located in the county jail. Inmates were recruited by the jail staff to lift me up the six steps and back down afterwards. "Don't tell these guys I'm a state lawyer," I whispered, only partly in jest.

The world of writing became much easier on the job. Once situated behind my desk, I had a speakerphone to handle the necessary phone calls and a standard office Dictaphone to record my legal efforts. With the microphone wedged under the edge of the desk blotter, the controls could be handled easily with my mouthstick. I could opine away in a medium I was comfortable with, my voice. When the transcript came back, I could add or delete or rearrange at will. During my years of service, I was blessed with the assistance of many capable and professional people. From my first legal secretary, Mary Ann Wippermann, to my last and longest serving one, Lucia Vest, I formed partnerships that allowed me to be very productive. My secretaries transcribed my work with ease and never complained about getting books from the library or running errands. The work product of any law firm, government or private, depends on the cooperation of many hands, from the mail clerk to the guy at the top. In my experience, legal secretaries are the best; my contributions would not have been possible without them.

Lucia Vest was much more than a secretary; she was a true administrative assistant. Actually, the army missed out on a great top sergeant when she became a secretary. During my years representing the Department of Revenue, she was the noncommissioned officer who kept our "unit" functioning smoothly. With a deadline looming, she knew how to command: "Listen up, Buddy Boy, if you think I'm going to stay late to finish your brief, you got another think coming. Stop lolly-gagging around and hop to it." Many younger associates, and I, responded immediately. We assumed she was kidding but it was safer to comply.

Lucia Vest at her command center.

I also learned who I could call if I needed something, from bathroom breaks, to lunch, to pushes to a meeting or to court. Most people seemed eager to help, or to drop by for conversation about legal issues or other matters. Sports talk at the office has always been a welcome diversion for men. Years later, as women entered the legal field in force, I was asked by a young female colleague why the men in the office seemed to bond so easily. It had been more difficult for her. I told her that one reason is that most men have one thing in common, a passion for sports. Later, I was amused to hear her talking football with the attorney down the hall.

During my tenure as an assistant attorney general, the attorney generals added staff routinely to handle an increasing work load. It was a bigger pool of potential helpers for me, but we soon outgrew our space in the Supreme Court Building. The division to which I was assigned was moved to an adjacent government building, the Broadway State Office Building. For the first time since I started, I could enter work through the front door. However, a court appearance meant trekking up a steep sidewalk past the front of the Supreme Court, followed by a steep descent along the side, and then up a very steep driveway to the back door.

The Broadway building was remodeled for use as a law office but the rooms were small. I didn't have to share my new office but it was so tiny that I had to sit with my back to the door. Later, the next attorney general procured the necessary funding to expand our offices to another floor and remodel the existing quarters again. To my delight, I was assigned a big corner office to roam around in; I even had chairs for visitors. During one of the remodeling projects, our division was asked to move to temporary offices several miles away. It meant finding a driver to get to court, but at least we could drive to the back door. Our temporary quarters were in a single story building, somewhat dilapidated, but adequate for our purpose. The only obstacle was a large curb that ran along the entire front. Instead of waiting for the Building and Grounds bureaucracy to remedy the situation, a colleague with some construction experience built a wooden ramp. He made it sturdy because my new wheelchair was heavier; it was motorized.

17

Ross Young

The doctor's notes in the file from my rehabilitation days at Warm Springs mentioned the possibility of a motorized wheelchair, **when** such technology became available. That vision became a reality for me more than a decade later. The developing space program produced many of the components necessary to make motorized chairs a practical reality. By the '60s, engineers where able to make use of the miniaturization of switches and other electrical parts developed for use in space to create compact but functional electric-powered wheelchairs. However, the chairs were of no use to me because I could not use the hand controls necessary to guide them. I continued to be pushed around in a manual chair, moving only by the grace of others.

Sometime during my law school days, I met the man who was to change all that. His name is Ross Young and he was a professor of mechanical engineering at the University of Missouri. The details of that meeting are lost in the mists of memory. Ross thinks we met through a physical therapist working at the University who wrenched my back so badly that I was sore for a week. I didn't need any more of that; my mission in Missouri was education, not pain. Anyway, Ross thinks she suggested to him that something should be done to make me more mobile. I recall meeting Ross through a dorm buddy who was an engineering student. No matter, the meeting was indeed fortuitous.

One of the classes taught by Ross was a practical engineering class with 18 students. As he tells the story, he addressed the class in this way: "Gentlemen. Our next class project will be an opportunity for you to use your engineering talents on a humanitarian level. Before you go out and make the big bucks, this will be a chance for you to use your skills to help somebody with a mobility problem." I became a class project.

Ross divided the class into two-man teams who were sent out to talk to me, and then to design something that would enable me to control a power wheelchair. They were forced to become physical therapists in some respect; they had to discover what muscles I could control and how well they moved against gravity without becoming fatigued. Armed with this information and the wiring diagram of a power wheelchair, they struggled to find a solution to the guidance problem.

Most of the proposals submitted by the teams were far-out and wildly imaginative, a combination of electronic and mechanical devices. Some relied on state-of-the-art components, all kinds of gizmos to do what I needed done electronically; others were simpler and more mechanical. As a whole, the designs gave new meaning to the term "over-engineered," they simply weren't practical. I needed something both simple and rugged; the simpler the better, the more rugged the better, and the less complicated the better. I would be the one using it, but the people who took care of me would have to be trained as well. I needed to be able to tell them how to assemble the system in the morning and disassemble it at night, without breaking something or getting something out of place.

Ross graded all of the designs for the students, and made notes of their findings. When I asked him which design was the best, he said: "Nobody's, if this is going to work, I'll have to do it myself." While I was silently questioning if it could be done at all, Ross was planning how to do it. He told me to buy a power wheelchair.

I lacked the resources to buy one but Dad found another source. Although no one in the family was a member, the Elks Club of Nebraska agreed to finance the purchase, provided I agreed to demonstrate my driving skill to them when the project was completed. Agreed! With financial assistance, I purchased an electric wheelchair, an early model Everest & Jennings. The standard guidance system was a four position joystick that was pushed in the direction the occupant desired to go. Using his plan, Ross broke the joystick into its individual components, using a microswitch for each motion: forward-left, forward-right, backward-left, and backward-right. He mounted the switches on a swiveling plate under my left foot because my strongest muscles were in the left foot and leg. Pushing down on the foot, I would activate the two front switches and move forward. Rocking back on my heel, I would activate the back two switches and move in reverse. If I flipped my leg to one side, I

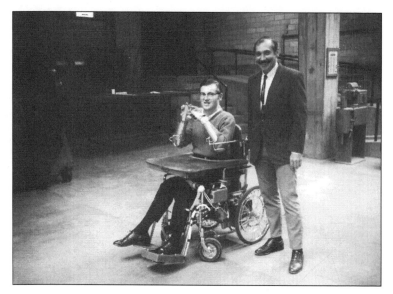

Ross Young and the First Miracle Machine

would activate one forward switch and one reverse switch to pivot and turn. Flipping my leg to the other side, I would pivot the other way. Ross' plan was workable; I drove the chair around the room the first time I was put in it. It was very, very clumsy, but it worked. With a great deal of fine-tuning, it worked even better.

To turn the chair on and off, Ross used a dimmer switch taken from the floorboard of a car. It was originally designed to dim the headlights of a car by stepping on it. He mounted it where I could hit it with my left knee. To soften the blow, he cut a toy red rubber ball in half, drilled a hole in it, and put it over the switch. It worked well. The last major problem involved flipping my left leg from side to side. Ross built a metal calf band to fit around the back of my leg and attached it to the foot plate, thereby stabilizing the ankle. That's when we discovered that the inner muscle wasn't strong enough. I could move my left knee out to activate the directional switches on the footplate, or to hit the dimmer switch, but I couldn't pull it back. We needed something elastic, something that could be tied to the wheelchair on one side and to the calf of my left leg on the other. It had to have the right amount of elasticity for me to push against it and yet strong enough to pull the knee back. After some thought, Ross decided to use the waistband from a pair of used underwear; you could even see the word "Jockey" on it. Another problem solved!

The chair adaptations were mostly made up of metal parts from his vast storehouse; Ross was a collector of discarded items. After rewiring all the circuitry and attaching the switches to the footplate, the final product had a raw look. All of the switches were exposed; Ross needed a cover. The rubber wastebasket in the corner was just the right size. He cut the bottom off the wastebasket, cut out the pattern for the foot, and mounted it over the entire footplate. With this cosmetic "improvement," I had a bright green cover over the wires and the switches under my left foot.

This process took many months to complete. We worked on it when our schedules permitted; the prospect of mobility kept me from getting too frustrated. Ross was always upbeat; he attacked each problem as it arose. With each fine-tuning, and practice time, I got more and more comfortable driving around. For the first time in my post-polio life I was mobile. By this time, I had graduated from law school and started my job. I decided it was time to go all out and abandon the manual chair. It caused quite a scene at the office. The freedom was exhilarating. I could leave my desk and visit with colleagues, or attend to business, without waiting for a push. With a little practice, I found I could master the elevator buttons with my mouthstick; I was free vertically as well as horizontally. I could move to my typewriter or I could back away from it; I could get to a telephone. If I wanted to move from the bedroom to the living room in my own apartment, I could do it myself. I could wander about outside on my own and at my own pace. The chair was best suited to level ground and smooth surfaces; I made sure I had somebody with me on the hilly Jefferson City sidewalks.

The chair kept running in the real world only because of Ross. I was always blowing out a switch or short circuiting something during my daily activities. "Ross, I am having trouble;" that was the beginning of frequent phone calls. His first question was always: "Are you still mobile?" If the answer was "No," he would drop everything, if possible, and rush to my rescue. I had a mechanic on call. Intermittent problems were the most difficult; they can be very frustrating. On those occasions, he would come at his earliest convenience. Ross often remarked: "I hate intermittent problems; if I see it smoking I know where the problem is, and then I can fix it."

After 11 years of this, I wanted something better. Wheelchair technology had been improving greatly and the newer models were more rugged and dependable. Ross agreed. He said the first chair was a prototype, an experiment; he wanted to build something that would get him out of the wheelchair business.

I purchased an Everest & Jennings 3P power chair; it had many improved features and much more power. Ross modified this one quite differently. Being Ross, he still used spare parts and spare pieces but he also utilized more stock parts, including the joystick itself so it could be serviced by wheelchair technicians. By positioning the joystick behind my left leg, he was able to build a mechanical system that allowed me to use the joystick by pushing the left foot up or down, or moving the left leg from side to side. It was much smoother than the old system and gave me better control of a more powerful chair. Ross galvanized the foot pedals to make it look more professional and less subject to rust, and even replaced the elastic "Jockey" strap with a metal spring. Instead of a dimmer switch, he installed a better "kill" switch on a hinged footplate under my right foot. Now both feet were involved.

Ross' skill at improvisation was beyond compare. The wheelchair industry has yet to produce a guidance system that could accommodate my needs. I have used this chair since 1982 with little input from Ross; he successfully engineered himself out of the wheelchair repair business.

As great an achievement as it was, I think that first motorized chair might have complicated my college days had I had it then. Looking back, it amazes me that I got through college, law school, and started a job without such freedom. However, I don't think my first power chair would have had the strength or the power to get to my classes soon enough, and I never lacked for willing hands to push me around in those days. Plus, it was much heavier; the added weight would have made negotiating steps and curbs more difficult. Lacking mobility forced me to concentrate on studies; there was nothing better to do. Also, motorized wheelchairs require a lot of care and feeding and that might have been difficult on a college budget. I've had to buy many batteries over the years and new motors. There is a lot of maintenance work on tires and wheels and bearings as well.

Ross came into the picture at just the right time. Mobility was essential on the job; it was also a boon to my post-college social life. However, I discovered that with mobility comes freedom, with freedom comes adventure, and with adventure comes danger. I was more cautious with the first chair but my range became much greater with the speed and the power of the 3P model. Once I gained confidence in the control system Ross designed for me, I was buzzing around town at every opportunity. On their frequent visits to Columbia, my parents were amazed by my jaunts. However, my offer to accompany Mom on walks to the mall or the grocery store was soon rejected. She found it too nerve-wracking to watch me zip down steep ramps or weave in and out of traffic.

My excursions were often in the company of a friend, Jim Crotts. Jim is a polio survivor too; his experience with electric wheelchairs is much deeper than mine. Any improvement that increased speed was soon brought to his attention; Jim claimed he had the fastest wheelchair in town, and he roamed great distances. His chair was his car. In fact, he once got a warning ticket from an overzealous cop. The cited offense: operating an unlicensed motor vehicle on a public street.

On one of our excursions, we misjudged the speed of an approaching thunderstorm and got caught in the rain. I was maintaining a steady pace in a tuck position to keep the rain out of my eyes when I heard this swooshing sound behind me. As he

Courtesy Katherine McHaney Coker

Strolling down the street with Jim Crotts

roared by, Jim screamed: "Wieler, you won't be any drier if I stay with you, I'm headed home." In a flash he disappeared into the raindrops, leaving me in his wake.

To someone in my condition, the threat of danger while cruising in a power chair is always present. Several incidents come to mind. On a quiet Saturday morning, Jim and I were driving down a slight hill on a side street when I discovered that I had no control over my chair. It was running straight and true with no guidance from me. I screamed out my problem and Jim came up with a quick solution. He planned to speed up to get in front of me and then slow down to catch my chair and force it to a halt. It worked! Once my chair bumped into his, the power cut off and I slid gently to the curb.

An inspection by a passerby revealed the problem; my helper had failed to securely attach the control rod to the back of the footplate and it slipped off. When he heard about our misadventure, my Cousin Bob asked the most pertinent question: "Why didn't you hit the 'kill' switch and let the motor resistance slow you down?" Truthfully, that never occurred to me; I was too paralyzed with fright. The lesson for me: Always stay focused when transferring in and out of the chair. If necessary, make someone check and recheck the attachments, even if it irritates them. The cost of any mishap falls on me.

On another occasion, my helper and I were doing laundry at a nearby shopping center. The controls had been sticking somewhat but not enough to concern me. As I turned the corner onto a sloping parking lot, I discovered, to my horror, that the controls were frozen. I was headed at full speed towards a parked car. Out of the corner of my eye I could see my helper running towards me in response to my screams. At the last moment he lunged between me and the car, absorbing the full impact of the chair. Mercifully, neither of us was injured but it cost $300 to remove the dent from the trunk of that lady's car. Again, I should have hit the "kill" switch but my brain was too busy preparing for pain. The lesson for me: Don't ignore problems with the guidance system; it's the only thing between me and disaster.

On two occasions, a front wheel broke off my chair. Both times I was barely moving on a level surface and nothing happened except for the inconvenience of getting back to bed so the problem could be fixed. The lesson for me: Sometimes I just get lucky; be grateful!

The most frightening incident happened at work. A coworker and I were returning to the office after a meeting in the State Capitol Building in Jefferson City. My colleague, Melodie Powell, and I were ambling down a wide sidewalk when I heard something snap. As the chair sped up, Melodie yelled: "Wieler, you're driving like an idiot."

"Melodie," I screamed back: "I'm out of control, stop me! Stop me!" Somehow, she ran me down and wrestled the chair to a stop before I could veer into a parking meter, a lamp post, a parked car, or even worse, hurtle into oblivion at the foot of St. Peter's Church. It was a remarkable feat, and certainly one not in her job description.

A wheelchair repairman discovered the problem; the shaft in the left side motor snapped from metal fatigue leaving me without control and at the mercy of gravity. In spite of frequent maintenance and repair, mechanical devices do break down and usually at the most inopportune time. My Uncle LeRoy refers to this as "the perversity of inanimate objects." Human intervention may save you, as it did me that day, but there's no guarantee. My active lifestyle required mobility, I had to be prepared to accept the consequences. Whining and crying, before or after, doesn't lessen the burden or ease the pain.

Several of my wheelchair mishaps were not the result of events beyond my control. One in particular was caused by my own stupidity. Within a few short years of receiving the gift of mobility, I was beginning to take it for granted. One spring night in Columbia, I was partying with my caregiver and some of our friends. During the course of the evening, I consumed entirely too much alcohol. It was a good party and I was enjoying it. Work was going well, my social life was improving, and I felt comfortable among my friends.

With little self-awareness, I slipped well past the warm and fuzzy feeling, that loose-tongue, uninhibited feeling, caused by a few drinks. I was feeling queasy. I slipped away and rolled down the sidewalk in search of a place to throw up. Although I'd been down that sidewalk hundreds of times, and was well aware of the eight inch drop-off on the left side as the walk neared the driveway, I was blissfully ignorant of the peril on this night.

Like a moth to the flame, I was drawn off the edge before I realized my mistake. It seemed like the ground came up to meet me as the wheelchair toppled off the sidewalk. I landed on my left side, still cradled inside the lapboard and the seat of the chair. Other than the shock of being flipped, I felt no pain. I could hear the right motor turning the rear wheel above me; I had this brief mental image of a prairie schooner flopping over in an old western movie, the rear wheel spinning helplessly in the air.

However, the situation was far from humorous. My lack of self-control had created a dangerous situation. Thankfully, relief was in sight. An angel was hovering nearby, and he spoke to me: "Are you all right?" A large black man was bending over me with a concerned expression on his face.

"I think so," I said; "can you find help to get me up?"

"I can do it myself," he declared and before I could respond I was back on four wheels. I recognized my hero as soon as I got a good look at him. It was Johnny Roland, a star athlete at

Missouri University during the mid-sixties, and later a successful player in the National Football League.

A quick check of my equipment revealed little damage. The feeder on the left side was bent slightly, causing my left arm to be elevated; my fingers were near my ear instead of in front of my face. By some miracle, I was still seated properly and the wheelchair responded to my commands.

"Are you hurt?" Johnny asked me as he brushed me off and straightened my shirt.

"No, I'm drunk," I replied.

With a laugh and a shake of his head, he departed. I never got the chance to thank him properly or ask him what brought him to Columbia and Gatehouse Apartments that night. Sobered considerably by my experience, I returned to the party.

"What happened to you?" was the common question.

"I just met Johnny Roland" was my reply.

I had more time to reflect the next morning. While nursing my headache and watching my caregiver bend my feeder back to its proper position, I was reminded of a quote from Uncle LeRoy: "Dick, when you have a hangover, you're really sick and nobody gives a damn." I learned a valuable lesson. Luckily, neither I nor my wheelchair had suffered any real damage, but my alcohol consumption could have been a disaster. Survival as an independent in my condition requires maintaining focus and control. It was foolish to impair both by getting drunk. Divine Providence saved me but I decided not to press my luck. I have an obligation too; it includes avoiding dangerous situations where humanly possible.

In spite of the setbacks and near catastrophes, both of my power chairs have been 98% or more effective. There were very few times when I was forced to cancel my plans or to stay home from work. Ross Young is largely responsible for that; his controls were solid and practical. I have difficulty putting my gratitude to him in words. A picture of us with that first chair is displayed in my living room. Over five years ago, I bought a new electric wheelchair to replace the current one but, despite the best efforts of some good people, it has yet to be modified successfully. We work on it periodically but the challenge is too great, especially when my old chair is still functional and comfortable. Ross just shakes his head when I discuss this with him; he dismisses it as over-engineered and needlessly complicated: "Why didn't you do what I did, why didn't you go with something mechanical?"

"Ross, because I don't have you around to do it," is my swift reply.

18

Real Life

The family sheltered me greatly during those long years of rehabilitation and college. They assumed so many burdens, leaving me free to pursue my goals. It was my turn to accept life's challenges. I had a regular job, a steady income, and an established routine for dealing with my disabilities. I was ready to embrace the twists and turns of real life.

Within a few months on the job at the attorney general's office, in late 1968, I received a frantic phone call from Mom. "Dick," she cried. "They're sending Mike to Vietnam, what can we do?" I fully suspected that would happen; my brother had enlisted in the Marines because a Marine recruiter convinced him that he would go there anyway once drafted and the Marines had an early discharge policy for those who served in a combat zone. "I can't stand the thought of losing another child," she said. I dashed off letters explaining our family situation to Nebraska's two Senators and the Congressman representing their district. By the time the letters filtered up the chain of command

and back, my brother was already "in country." Word came back from his commanding officer that Mike was offered the opportunity to serve elsewhere but refused. He wasn't being noble, he said, he just wanted to do his duty and get out of the Corps as soon as possible.

It was a very long year. I tried to avoid the daily news as much as I could, preferring to concentrate on my job instead. The pent-up anxiety burst like a balloon with the news that Mike was coming home. He was scheduled to arrive in St. Louis after a brief layover in California. I was waiting at Lambert Field when he came through the gate. The terminal was crowded with young men in uniform; Mike was one of many in his khaki outfit. He was much thinner than I remembered and quite pumped up about being home. He refused to leave the airport before he walked around most of the terminal. "I want the other guys in uniform to see my green Vietnam service ribbon," he said. I asked a few general questions about his year in Vietnam, nothing more. It was a closed subject.

The Vietnam War was one of the defining moments for my generation. While young men were fighting and dying over there, social unrest was roiling our society at home. The war was a heated topic of conversation everywhere. Many years after it ended, I read an article in the Columbia newspaper about the "Moving Wall." It is a smaller mobile replica of the Vietnam Memorial in Washington, D.C. To my knowledge, it is still touring the country. It was being exhibited in a nearby town, and I was determined to see it. My neighbor, Terry, was from that town and I asked him to go with me. On the drive over, we

My brother Mike, *semper fi, "always faithful."*
And that is what he has been.

talked about the war and the impact it had on our lives. I was astonished when Terry said he didn't know anybody whose name was inscribed on the Wall.

With the help of a friendly guide, I looked for three names. The names are grouped under the year in which each soldier fell. The first was a young man from the old farm neighborhood; the second was Irv's youngest brother who was killed three weeks after entering the country; the third was Charlie, dear Charlie. Charles Schwartz was a young man from rural Missouri who arrived at the dorm in the fall of 1964. Quiet and unassuming, Charlie was everybody's friend. We spent the next four years together, two in the dorm and two off campus. After graduation, Charlie and his girlfriend headed for California. Some months later, I received a letter from him saying that he had enlisted in the army. My last letter to Charlie was returned unopened from the Defense Department along with a note expressing sympathy that the letter could not be delivered; Sergeant Schwartz had been killed in action.

For those of us at the Moving Wall that day, it was a somber moment. I didn't sense any bitterness, just a quiet sorrow; even the children seemed subdued. The loss of potential represented on that wall was overwhelming. Perhaps Clint Eastwood said it best in the movie, *Unforgiven*, when he told a young would-be gunslinger: "When you kill somebody, you not only destroy what he is, you destroy everything he might become." Given the nature of mankind, wars are often unavoidable; they are never acceptable.

My brother came home; his war was over. Mom said he didn't volunteer much information about his experience. He did give her one instruction: "If you want something when I'm sleeping, just yell; don't ever touch me." After several months at home, he began sleeping in his bed again instead of huddled in

Family Portrait in the '70s

the corner under his camouflage blanket.

I got the word that summer that he and his high school sweetheart, Beverly, were getting married. He told Mom that he was ready, and getting tired of having to drive home after dates. They were married in November of 1970; I managed to get home for the wedding. My oldest niece, Kari, was born in early 1972 and followed 14 months later by her sister, Marci. Mom and Dad were finally grandparents.

These were truly joyful events, tempered for me by the fact that my professional lifestyle and independent life was slowly separating me from my family and their rural lifestyle. In 1975, I got another phone call from my mother. "Dick, Kari's in the hospital; the doctors think she has cancer," she cried.

"How can this be?" I thought, "She's only three years old." The doctors were right. Kari was suffering from a Wilm's

Tumor, a rare form of cancer that strikes the kidney, usually in young children. Separated by distance and work responsibilities, there was nothing I could do. She was in good hands with cancer specialists in Omaha and surrounded by a loving family. I was on the outside, looking in. All I could say was "keep me informed."

In the months that followed, Kari was subjected to surgery, cobalt radiation treatments, and chemotherapy. One kidney was destroyed but she survived. Many trips to Omaha for periodic chemotherapy were required over the next few years. Mom says she was one brave little girl. When it was time for a treatment, she would march down the hall and enter the treatment room all by herself. When it was over, she'd march back out, refusing to talk to anybody, even her "Gumpy." Gumpy was the name she gave Dad before she could pronounce grandfather; somehow it stuck. The silence would continue for about half the trip home and then she was her usual happy self.

I missed many family things. The girls grew up with an absentee uncle, the one who was there only during the Christmas Holiday. My world was so delicately balanced by my professional duties and my personal needs that it needed my constant attention to avoid chaos. Happily, Kari confounded her doctors in many ways; the list of things they said could never happen diminished over the years. Her ability to get pregnant was the most astonishing; she and her husband are raising four healthy children. She is still one brave woman, having beaten back another round of cancer, breast cancer this time.

Marci has also grown up. She was the family "free spirit," dreaming of adventure in far-off places during her youth. She

My nieces on the day of Kari's wedding

made it as far as Texas before settling down in Nebraska, an hour from West Point. Marci is one of my favorite people; she has an engaging and outgoing personality. "Little Miss Sunshine," if you will; she makes me laugh. She and her husband have two lively little boys who, at an early age, are showing a passion for sports. Raising them will be her greatest adventure.

During the late '70s, Dad and Mike formed a farming partnership; Mike bought a small house in West Point for the folks and he moved his family to the farm. Another generation was taking up farming as an occupation. I asked Mom if she would miss farm life. She surprised me with her answer: "Dick, I never looked back as we drove out the driveway; that place has held bad memories for me since you kids got sick in 1955." My parents were now townspeople. Dad did what he could to make the house more accessible for my visits, and Mom planted flowers. She loves her flowers.

"Dick, your father is on the line," was the word from my secretary as I was chatting with a colleague in the hallway. That's odd I thought, my dad rarely calls me at home and never at the office. The year was 1984. President Reagan's economic policies were beginning to take effect; interest rates and inflation were starting to come down. It seemed like the good times were in. I was too busy with my world to keep up with farm and commodity prices; I assumed the partnership would be profitable. Despite the economic ups and downs, the farm had always provided a living for the family.

"What's up, Pop," I said.

"Dick," he said, "the bank wants to take the farm. Can you help us?"

"What!" I asked. As I recovered from the initial shock, he told me that livestock prices were down again and that they'd had a round of bad luck with stock losses and animal diseases. I got as much information as I could and promised to get back to him. Then I called the loan officer at his local bank.

The answer was simple according to the bank. My dad and brother were overextended on loans and the farm's value wasn't sufficient to cover the debt. Borrowed money is a fact of life in the livestock business; I wasn't surprised that they had debts.

"Why did you continue to loan money when the business wasn't making a profit?" I asked the man.

"Because the value of the land was sufficient at the time to cover the loans, and the bank believed in their ability to make money in the cattle market," he answered. "Things are different now, the markets are bad and land prices have fallen perceptibly in the past year; we need to foreclose to protect our interests." I couldn't believe this.

"Do you need to take the whole farm? Wouldn't parts of it satisfy the debt?" I asked.

"No, we need all of it," he replied.

My legal education wasn't going to solve this problem; we needed money and lots of it. I wasn't in a position to finance it by myself. My dad had asked his big shot lawyer son for help and I was about to let him down.

"Dad, the only answer here is bankruptcy," I told him in my return phone call. He flatly refused to even consider that, and neither would my brother. If that was the only option, the bank could take the farm. He and Mike were determined to settle their debts without declaring bankruptcy.

That was it. The farm which had been in the family for three generations was signed over to the bank. The Wieler's were no longer land holders. Mike found a house to rent and started driving a truck to pay off the remaining debts and feed his family. I bought the house in town so the folks would have a place to live. I've often wondered how Dad dealt with the loss; I'm sure it broke his heart, but Mom told me that he took it in stride. One thing about my father, he never looked back. "What's past is past," he'd say.

"Will you have enough to live on without the farm?" was my question.

"We'll get by," Mom said. "Your dad and I grew up during the Great Depression and we struggled to get by for years on the farm. We know how to live frugally." I believed her. With Social Security and some financial assistance from me, they did get by.

Grandma John spent her last two years at home with my parents. Her family visits had become a thing of the past; her health was starting to decline. She died in March of 1986. Cousin Bob and I returned home for the funeral. The minister's eulogy was very personal and very moving; the story of Grandma's life of sacrifice, dignity, and courage was retold for the mourners. The service ran long because of the many family tributes; we were reluctant to part with her and give her back to the husband who had died so long ago. Names, dates, and inscriptions on headstones do not tell the stories of those neither blessed nor cursed by History's fame. Grandma John was our family treasure; she set the standard for us to follow. On the occasions when I failed to meet that standard, I knew she would be the last to chide me for it.

I lived a professional's life for over twenty years. The money I earned helped buy better clothes, better furniture, and better vehicles. It allowed me to set aside savings and provide some funds to my family in times of need. More importantly, it allowed me to be self-sufficient. I have no wish to relive that busy life in detail with a memory fogged by time. The cases I handled are a matter of public record; all appellate cases are recorded in case-law books designed specifically for that purpose. My legal experiences and my approach to my job were nicely summarized in two letters I wrote, one in 1973, and one in 1988. Both letters were in response to inquiries from law students with disabilities.

January 15, 1973

Dear Miss Wiener,

Please accept my apologies for my tardiness in responding to your letter. I have just returned from a short vacation trip and have been trying to catch up on some of the work which has piled up.

It is hard to explain your experiences and problems when you start thinking about them. I really can't say to what extent my failures and shortcomings can be attributed to physical handicaps and to what extent my successes have been achieved in spite of physical handicaps.

I graduated from law school in 1968. I have had no success whatsoever in obtaining a job in the private practice of law. I have interviewed several law firms and have always come away with a feeling that they really were not interested in hiring someone as extensively involved physically as I am. My one and only job has been with the Attorney General's office in Missouri.

To a large extent, I am very much satisfied with government work. The pay is getting better and the hours are reasonable, especially for one who does not have the physical stamina to work the hours that are sometimes required of a person in private practice. My work has been varied, interesting, and on occasion, highly legal. I have appeared at hearings before administrative tribunals, argued cases before appellate courts in this state, and, at times have appeared in various circuit courts for the purpose of arguing motions and presenting evidence. However, moving around does present a problem and the best part about this job is the amount of work that can be produced without leaving the office building. Since the office has a large staff, it has been easy to find help for grabbing books and other research materials. I make extensive use of a Dictaphone and utilize a no hands or loudspeaker telephone. Also, the acquisition of an electric wheelchair has been invaluable.

It seems to me that the hardest thing is getting hired by somebody, anybody. I have been told that my boss did not regret hiring me, but that he had serious doubts about the success of the venture initially. If you can handle college and law school, you can handle a job. It is simply a matter of convincing someone to take that first step.

I hope these rambling thoughts are helpful.

Sincerely,

Richard L. Wieler

The second letter:

March 14, 1988

Dear Ms. Akerson:

I have tried to respond as best I can to the questions posed in your letter. I have worked for the State of Missouri since September, 1968. As a member of the Attorney General's office, I have been assigned to the Department of Revenue and I represent the Director in legal disputes involving taxes, motor vehicles, and driver's licenses. I also provide legal advice to several other state agencies, some of which involves litigation.

I was diagnosed as a victim of polio in September of 1955. As a result, I am a quadriplegic with some breathing impairment. There is little doubt that my disability affects my relationships with others, including clients, attorneys, co-workers, or judges. I try to deal with it by acknowledging that it is a problem but that it's my problem, not theirs. I feel that it is my responsibility to put them at ease and I do so, if possible, by discussing the issues which brought us together in the first place. If one can demonstrate some knowledge and good humor without dwelling on his shortcomings, I have found that most people are willing to give you a chance if you can demonstrate ability.

I have never had a jury trial but there are always problems (or challenges) to someone in this profession. I have a tremendous problem dealing with the large volume of paper and the books which are part of legal practice. In court, I find myself relying on memory in order to avoid the hassle of checking through notes or reviewing documents. In my opinion, a physical disability can never be an asset unless you are seeking welfare payments. It has not aided me unless you count the fact that I take my job seriously because I cannot make any money digging ditches.

Sincerely yours,

Richard L. Wieler

19

Relationships

The first year in the Missouri Attorney General's office was a challenge, but the transition from student to employee had been successful. In many ways, work was easier than law school, and I got paid for it. Since moving back to Columbia in early 1969, I had greater success in finding and holding caregivers/ roommates, and the social scene was much better. The four months spent in Jefferson City had been lonely ones for me. Although I lived within minutes of the office, the after-work hours had been boring indeed. My colleagues were mostly older and married with lives of their own, and I was confined to my apartment in a manual wheelchair.

Many positive things had happened since my move back to Columbia. The presence of a large university and two small colleges give Columbia a more youthful atmosphere. Plus, the University of Missouri was a great outlet for major college sports; I love sports. Also, Columbia was more accessible. The large influx of disabled students to the University seemed to spur the entire community into removing architectural barriers. Thanks to Ross Young, I had a motorized wheelchair to take better advantage of those opportunities. The 35-mile commute posed no problem; I found many colleagues who were willing to drive my van. A number of people found the social life in Columbia much better even though their jobs were located in the State's capitol city. I supplied the van and they supplied the driving and chipped in for gas.

My job at the Missouri Attorney General's Office had become more exciting as well. The general election in November of 1968 produced a major surprise. The incumbent who hired me, Norman Anderson, had been ousted by a young Republican from St. Louis, John (Jack) Danforth. Jack was the first Republican elected to state-wide office in Missouri in three decades; it marked the beginning of political change for the State. Missouri was becoming a two-party state again. At the time this meant nothing to me, my concern was whether I'd keep the job I had begun just two months earlier. Assistant attorney generals serve at the pleasure of their elected boss. Changes began in earnest with Jack's swearing-in ceremony in January of 1969. Many of my old colleagues had resigned by then; they were political animals anyway and had no interest in serving a Republican.

I didn't consider myself a political appointment; I was trying to be a good lawyer. Mr. Danforth brought a fresh outlook to the office. His often stated goal was to make the Missouri Attorney General's Office into a first class law office and not just another political arm of government. When he offered me re-appointment, he made it clear that I was to devote myself to legal matters and leave the political decisions to him. That was fine with me; I never saw myself as a politician.

Over the next year, Jack re-energized the office. He hired many new attorneys with differing backgrounds and skills to compliment the holdovers. I was comfortable with my new colleagues from the very beginning. By the fall of 1970, the office had become a cohesive unit and I had made some dear and lasting friendships. My work load had increased steadily as well; I was becoming adept at the practice of government law.

Still, something was missing. Although my contacts with my colleagues included social events outside of the office, they all had wives or girlfriends. I wanted that too. I had learned how to cope with my paralysis, I had gotten an education and a job, I was earning enough money to be self-sufficient, and yet I was alone. Polio had done nothing to stifle my sex drive; it was remarkably healthy. In spite of earlier reservations about pursuing romance, it seemed that female companionship was the next step towards normality; the normality I so desperately craved.

I can be very shy around women. I'm never sure how they might react to my condition and I was totally unprepared for the practice of romance. Sexuality was never a topic of discussion during the rehabilitation process, not even with the staff psychologist at Warm Springs. The Catholic instruction of my youth stressed spirituality; physical desires were to be suppressed upon pain of damnation. Getting an education and learning to live independently left no time for socialization.

During my college years, the '60s generation changed the moral landscape of America. Their challenge to authority sparked by protests to the war in Vietnam had rapidly spread into all aspects of life, including sex. "Make love, not war," they shouted. "Sex, drugs, and rock and roll" was the rallying cry. Pop culture was quick to join the trend as movies and song lyrics became more sexually explicit. Magazines devoted to sex entered the mainstream and prior restrictions on pornography were relaxed by judicial decisions invoking the constitutional doctrine of freedom of speech. America was overwhelmed by this newest secular movement. Religion and tradition, the normal standard bearers of morality, seemed powerless to stop it. Freed from the fear of unwanted pregnancy by the invention of the birth control pill and encouraged by the rise of modern feminism, women were being urged to explore their sexual natures. "Sex is good," said the modern prophets. "Those who warn about the dangers are simply trying to deny you of your pleasures." Within a few years these harbingers of "good" times would achieve their greatest triumph as the U.S. Supreme Court handed down its decision in *Roe v. Wade*. In a single decision America erected its greatest monument to selfishness; millions of the defenseless were to be aborted because they were inconvenient.

I took my first plunge into a relationship in the midst of this swirling maelstrom of social revolt. In the fall of 1970, I was watching the incoming tenants to the complex from my vantage point on the passageway outside my apartment. September was always a time of frenzied activity when university students moved in for the start of the fall semester. As usual, I was on the lookout for future caregivers or new friends. Soon I was on good speaking terms with three co-eds who moved in three doors down. One of them in particular seemed very friendly. We started spending more time together; I looked forward to talking to her after work every day and on the weekends. She was a slender young woman with long, straight, dark hair and round wire-rimmed glasses in the hippie fashion of the day. She was a senior at the University, majoring in special education.

I knew how to talk to people about a lot of things; I knew nothing about talking to a young woman. My approach must have been very awkward but she didn't seem to mind. Our conversations became more personal and lasted longer into the night with each passing week. Because of her graceful but steady approach, we became more intimate. Where my physical condition forced me to be passive, she gently took the aggressor's role. I couldn't believe my luck; this beautiful young woman had become part of my life. I was in love. As spring approached, I had dreams of marriage, a home, and children. My agonizing road back to normal life would soon be complete, in spite of the disabilities. How naïve I was.

In spite of every desperate ploy I could think of, our relationship cooled quickly. It turns out she was dreaming too: of graduate school in Arizona, of living in the mountains, of other guys. Whatever she felt for me and the things we had done together, they weren't sufficient to alter any of her plans. She withdrew from my world very quickly; I'm not that hard to avoid. By semester's end, she had moved to another part of town and I never saw her again.

I was crushed. I hadn't realized that relationships could reach such an intimate level without commitment. Obviously, she didn't feel the same as I did. Her final thoughts on our relationship were relayed to me months later by a mutual acquaintance: "I never meant to hurt him. He seemed so alone; I felt sorry for him. I thought his life would improve if he started dating."

At last, the truth lay before me. In my hunger for romance, I had mistaken pity for love. She never loved me. Looking back, I'm amazed at my innocence, or was it ignorance? My focus had been a dogged determination to succeed on a lasting basis; the notion of a casual encounter seemed alien. Our time together might have been better spent had I known that she viewed it as "just dating." In some way, we were both victims of my fantasies. The bitter taste of failure stayed with me for months. Thankfully, I had a job to do. My responsibilities at the office kept me from wallowing in a perpetual state of self-pity. With time the pain ceased.

My notions of love and commitment were jolted by my first encounter with modern romance. My views had been rooted in the experiences of my family. My parents were married for 67 years before Dad died in January of 2006. They looked to each other for love, support, and encouragement throughout their marriage. It sustained them through bad times and good. Yet, in the psycho-babble culture of the day, that was called "co-dependency." Who would have thought that what I considered the essence of marriage was a bad thing? A good relationship in modern lexicon seemed to be nothing more than a contract among equals; each party retains the right to do whatever he or she chooses to do. Worse, if either party is dissatisfied for any reason, the commitment can be broken, even the solemn vow of marriage. Given my circumstances, how could I ever bring an equal share to a relationship? A quadriplegic individual by definition is co-dependent. Yet, I'm the one who broke off my next attempt at love. Several years had passed after my brief love affair with the co-ed. My best friend, Irv Friedhoff, had forsaken the private practice of law in favor of government service and had moved into the apartment next door. With each other for company and an increasing circle of friends, our social life was expanding even more. However, the need for companionship still occupied my mind. The opportunity came when one of our neighbors abandoned Columbia for his native Texas, leaving behind his job and a girlfriend. Cut adrift, she became a regular visitor to our social gatherings. She was a welcome addition, first as a friend and later much more.

Things were different this time. My heart was hardened by my prior experience; I didn't want to be the object of another social experiment. I needed to believe she was looking for commitment as much as I was. Over the course of the next year, things progressed to the point where I asked her to marry me and she agreed. That's when second thoughts intruded. Now that I had her answer, I realized that marriage to this woman was more than I wanted to handle. We were better suited to friendship. With the exception of Irv, she didn't like my circle of friends. She didn't see the reason to share me with a bunch of people she felt uncomfortable around; I couldn't abandon the lifestyle that provided me with a level of security. Other differences, once mere distractions, suddenly became barriers. For one thing, I was becoming more intrigued with history and politics; she was totally indifferent. She devoured mystery and romance novels; I've never liked them. Actually, we had very little in common; we simply drifted apart. We remain friends to this day. She chides me softly on occasion about my marriage proposal, but I think we both realize it would have been a mistake. My proposal was forsaken with little sadness on my part. I was steadily becoming less sure about marriage.

My need to surround myself with as many people as possible to function successfully seemed to run counter to the basic philosophy of marriage. The theory of two functioning as one didn't fit. Anyone marrying me would be forced to accept a host of strangers in her household, or assume the entire role as caregiver. It would have taken a special person indeed to meet all of my needs herself.

However, forsaking marriage didn't mean abandoning female companionship, or so I thought. After all, I was living in this brave new world where old traditions like marriage could be discarded as relics of the past. Still, my sporadic encounters over the next few decades were hardly fulfilling. Mostly, I met women who were badly bruised by former relationships, or busy pursuing their careers. The "if it feels good, do it" theme of modern culture has claimed so many victims. The ones I met were hurt by divorce, or saddled with drug problems, or haunted by a bad childhood.

On the positive side, my lack of success in this area was tempered by the increasing responsibilities of my job. In this arena I was a success and I took great pride in my work. Jack Danforth had moved on to the U.S. Senate and his successor, John Ashcroft, invited me back to the Attorney General's Office. I had left the office to pursue other opportunities working directly for the Missouri Department of Revenue and the Public Service Commission. For three years I worked with administrators instead of lawyers and courts. It had been a mistake. I belonged in the Attorney General's Office and John's offer was gratefully accepted.

With almost ten years of experience, I was ready to assume greater responsibility. John asked me to be the lead attorney representing the Department of Revenue. My job was simply put: "Dick," he said; "I want you to take control of our legal duty to represent the Department. Taxes are the life blood of government, but I don't want to be involved directly. I expect you to be the face of this office when it comes to all matters involving revenue."

Thus was born my legal calling. For over a decade I, with the help of several younger associates, represented the interests of the Department of Revenue in various administrative hearings, circuit courts and the Missouri Supreme Court. John's successor, Bill Webster, maintained the status quo. I had earned the trust of my bosses; I was allowed to conduct the Department's legal affairs with little or no direct intervention.

My work consumed a great deal of my time, leaving little opportunity to obsess over the lack of female companionship. But my health was beginning to deteriorate by the end of the '80s. The need for assistance dealing with chronic hypoventilation had occurred several years ago. With aging, my weak diaphragm was increasingly unable to handle breathing needs. One of the proposed remedies was a return to the iron lung. As that horrific thought rattled around in my brain, the little angels came to the rescue again. A respiratory therapist in Columbia advised me to contact a pulmonary specialist in St. Louis, Doctor Oscar Schwartz. Oscar introduced me to the latest ventilation equipment, a small portable device that would breathe for me through a nasal mask. Using it every night allowed my diaphragm to rest completely. It was a small price to pay as I was able to resume my job and my independent lifestyle.

Other complications forced a different outcome in 1990. A series of intestinal maladies required me to take an extended sick leave in 1989. The diagnosis was murky at best, alternatively described as diverticulitis, ulcerative colitis, or irritable bowl syndrome. Whatever, the medicine prescribed to control the situation was a powerful appetite suppressant.

I returned to work in the fall, much weakened by my ailment. Somehow I managed to press on with work as my condition slowly deteriorated. As the new year began, it was obvious that I couldn't continue. I was so weak that speech was barely audible, a bad problem for a lawyer. On February 2, 1990, I made my last appearance before the Missouri Supreme Court, somehow I knew there would never be another day in court for me. At issue was an important state income tax dispute with interstate complications. It was possibly my worst performance ever. After oral arguments were concluded, my colleague drove me to St. Louis and an appointment with Doctor Oscar. He admitted me to the hospital immediately.

I had lost over fifty pounds dealing with my condition; my stamina was shot. After consultation with the staff gastroenterologist and an extensive intestinal exam, Oscar was convinced that the medicine was part of the problem. But, whatever the cause, the fact remained that I was too weak to return to work and the prognosis for a return to my former status was guarded. I was advised to cut back, seek relief from the stress of my work, and prepare to become more ventilator dependent. There was no guarantee that the diaphragm would regain the strength necessary to allow me to breathe independently during the day.

The return to my apartment in Columbia was somber indeed. The prospect of giving up my occupation was devastating. It was a large part of my safety net; my colleagues had become an integral part of my daily care. Thankfully, the health insurance coverage provided by the State came to the rescue. In order to keep me out of the hospital, it was decided that thirteen hours of skilled home care per day was the best option. With this system in place I was able to stay home and maintain my independence. As the weeks stretched into months, I regained some weight and strength. The hours spent in solitude gave me time to reflect on the rigors of my job. The stress had been much greater than I realized. It was time to face the new reality; my physical condition would not allow a return to work. At age fifty, my contribution to America's work force was over.

The desire for companionship resurfaced and became more intense as I settled into premature retirement. I pursued every woman I could in my limited circumstances with the hope that someone would ease the emptiness, the loneliness. I was trapped in the web of my own desire. The more I struggled, the greater the pain. Was I not good enough? It seemed to me that I was a life raft to some of the women I met and yet they chose to swim with the sharks. Some pop psychologists offer the following advice on relationships: "Never get involved with someone who has bigger problems than you do." Was that it? My problems were obvious but I thought I had demonstrated my ability to deal with them. This was one hurdle I couldn't clear, no matter how hard I tried. A successful relationship requires two people and I wasn't getting any cooperation.

This longing remained in the forefront for several years as the transformation from working attorney to quiet retiree took place. My former colleagues continued with their busy lives; we saw less and less of each other. My health had stabilized at an acceptable level but I knew I could never push myself again. Although I missed my former comrades and the real world I left behind, the job itself was no longer important. I had done my best and I was content to leave the stress to others. The world I now occupied was more like a soap opera, pursuing love and companionship only to be rejected time after time.

At night that little voice in my head kept growing louder: "Dick Wieler, where's your pride? You have little patience for those who feel sorry for you and yet you're indulging in self-pity."

"But I didn't volunteer to live a monastic life," I whined.

"You didn't ask for paralysis either," said the little voice. "In life's card game, you don't control the deck. You play the cards you're dealt to the best of your ability and accept the outcome. Whining is for losers, deal with it."

Much as I hated to admit it, my little voice was right. I was not dealing with reality. I needed to step back and take a hard look at the social culture around me, and my unwitting acceptance of it. It didn't take genius to see that the leaders of the sexual revolution were wrong. Although they were, and still are, in denial; the consequences of casual sex in our society are truly shocking. At the very least, there are issues of self-worth or self-esteem if you discover your partner is less committed than you, or shopping around for a better deal. The feeling of being used is never pleasant. Even worse, the past four decades have seen dramatic increases in illegitimate births, divorces, children in one parent homes, sexually transmitted diseases including the deadly AIDS, and over thirty million abortions and still counting. There's no such thing as casual sex.

It hadn't brought the love and commitment I truly wanted. Sex is one of the most powerful gifts given us by God; unfortunately it is also His greatest challenge. It co-exists with so many rivals: pride, envy, greed, jealousy, selfishness, lust, and even hate. In my opinion, avoiding the pitfalls requires a belief in a higher purpose, and a higher power. Perhaps that's the reason for the challenge. I'm not a preacher and I apologize for sounding like one. However, in my humble opinion, a loving and faithful marriage is the safest place to exercise the gift.

However, a close relationship is not the only way to a happy and productive life. I chased that dream diligently, thinking it was the last link in my fight for normality. I wanted so badly to share my life with a close companion like so many others have. I wish that dream had come true; I consider it my greatest failure. However, there is no comparison between loneliness and being alone. Loneliness is a state of mind, a belief that nothing worthwhile can come from being alone. Yet, logic and experience tells me that this is simply not true.

Life is the greatest gift a person can be given. It comes with so many options that the failure or refusal to exercise any one of them never diminishes the gift itself. Every one has regrets about something in his past, but life should be a celebration of accomplishments, not failures. Life's harvest for me has been bountiful. Despite the failures, the setbacks, and the dreams unfulfilled, I've never had to look far to find someone carrying a heavier burden than I ever have. I am sustained by the gifts placed in my path.

20

Back to the Beginning

As the spring of 2003 rolled in, my delicately balanced world was beginning to crumble. It had been thirteen years since my health mandated early retirement. The network of friends and colleagues built up so carefully over my working years had all but vanished. They were busy with their work and their lives; I was no longer part of that world.

Some of us still got together sporadically for "movie night," a tradition begun years ago as a means of critically reviewing a movie over pizza and a few beers. We usually set up shop at my buddy Irv's apartment next door. Over the years, the movie became less important; it was an excuse to get together and discuss the issues of the day. It was my chance to find out what was happening in my former workplace. I had long since stopped dropping by the office. Jefferson City seemed so far away and I was so completely out of the loop.

Thankfully, my condition had stabilized. The arrangement with the state's health insurance program, guaranteeing thirteen hours of home health care every day, was sufficient to keep me from lapsing back into the prior difficulties. However, my breathing was a continuing problem. I was becoming more ventilator dependent with aging and my former stamina would never return.

The home health care was provided by a private company under contract with the state health insurance provider. At first, this seemed like a wonderful arrangement; I was no longer responsible for finding my own caregivers. This removed a great deal of stress and uncertainty on my part. The company did all the screening and had backup available should someone not be able to work a shift. However, as the years slid by, this arrangement lost some of its appeal because of the inconsistent quality of the caregivers and the frequent turnover. I was becoming increasingly frustrated by this as I became more and more dependent on home health care.

Other things were happening that spring to make my situation less certain. Irv had retired from his job and was becoming more restless with life in Columbia and his cramped apartment. He had built a house in his small Iowa hometown and talked of spending more time there. He called it a vacation home but I feared it would become much more with time. The thought of living in Columbia without Irv next door to watch my back was disconcerting, to say the least.

Also, Mom and Dad were reaching an age where travel was becoming complicated. They had been faithful visitors since my retirement, often staying for weeks at a time during holidays and special occasions. This was a great comfort to me as my traveling abilities were limited by my condition. During their last visit, Dad volunteered that he wasn't up to that four-hundred-mile trip much longer. He was approaching his eighty-seventh birthday, his right knee was shot, and his general health was slowly eroding. His old Chrysler wasn't in any better shape.

It was time for a change; it was time to go home. The more I thought about it, the more I came to that conclusion. I wanted to spend more time with my parents, I wanted to reconnect with my family, and I no longer had any excuse for living in Columbia. Although life in Missouri had been exciting and fulfilling, those days were history and I felt the need to be closer to those who loved me. Columbia was becoming a lonely place.

I began making plans for the move. The state health-insurance provider assured me they would work with a home health-care agency in Nebraska. My access to home health care would not be altered. The excitement in the family was palpable when I told them of my decision. During a short visit to find a place to live and to arrange home health care, my Aunt Vernice, Dad's sister, told me it was about time. "You've missed so many family things already," she said.

I decided to move into an independent living facility within a mile of Mom and Dad's house. This seemed like the most practical choice for me. We would still be close, but I could remain independent in a place of my own. The facility sits on ground formerly occupied by the old hospital; I was literally returning to the place of my birth. Looking out the window, I could even see the school grounds where I played as a child.

The director of nursing at the facility was concerned about my obvious lack of mobility but the administrator was convinced that I had demonstrated a remarkable level of independence over the course of my life. An apartment suitable to my needs was being remodeled; it would be available in the fall.

After my decision, Irv decided to return permanently to his hometown. His house was ready and waiting and he said there was no point remaining in Columbia with me leaving. Irv's lease expired in July, mine at the end of August. I was left with an empty feeling the day he moved out. It was a preview of what lay in store for me as I watched his family load up their rental truck.

The month of August seemed to drag initially. My friends and former colleagues threw a big farewell party at a local watering hole; the place was packed. It was a heart warming evening. It made me even more conscious of what I was leaving behind. With memories like this, my forty years in Missouri had been well spent indeed.

I left Missouri on Labor Day weekend of 2003. My brother and sister-in-law supervised the loading of our rental truck. It didn't look like much as they carried my accumulated material goods from the apartment. The apartment itself looked worn and shabby devoid of furniture. As I looked around one last time, I could hardly believe that I had spent over half of my life in this small space.

The ride home was somber. Although it seemed like the right decision, there was no great feeling of joy in this homecoming. I just knew I had run out of reasons to stay in Columbia. My Aunt Vernice's words were on my mind. I had missed too many family events; the latest was her funeral. She died of cancer in July before my return.

Settling down to life in West Point was difficult. I kept trying to compare it to the past in Missouri. That was unfair of course; my condition precluded a return to that lifestyle. Still, I was a restless spirit. West Point was dull indeed compared to the life I'd led.

With time, I adjusted to the new situation. Among the biggest positives was a better and more consistent group of caregivers. Also, watching nature at work is very comforting; the Nebraska countryside has always seemed beautiful to me. I spent a lot of time just cruising through the softly rolling hills that seem to float endlessly to the horizon. Most importantly, I spent time with my parents. Until my return, I hadn't realized their level of concern over my living conditions in Columbia, even though I had done my best to avoid the details. They were elated to have their oldest chick close to their wing; and I was able to make improvements to their house because of the opportunity to make closer inspections.

As time passed, it became increasingly clear that Dad's health was slipping. He went from a cane to a walker during my first year at home. His right knee caused him a great deal of pain but he thought he was too old for replacement surgery. As long as he could hobble off to his afternoon card games, he'd deal with the pain. I made myself useful by taking them to various doctor appointments and reviewing their medications; they both grumbled about the number of pills they were prescribed. However, in spite of the obvious aging, they were still quite active in my opinion.

I'd been home for two years when things turned ugly. Dad was complaining about stomach pains but refused to go to the

Kevin Gall Photography

Last family photo: Mom & Dad's 65th Anniversary

doctor before his regularly scheduled appointment in November. His doctor feared the worst immediately and ordered a CAT scan. The scan revealed a pancreatic cancer that was spreading rapidly. Dad was referred to a specialist who confirmed the diagnosis and offered little hope. Because Aunt Vernice had died of the same type of cancer two years earlier, we knew it was terminal. Like his sister, Dad refused treatment. He died on January 30, 2006.

I'm so grateful for the time I had to spend with him. I'm even more grateful for the time I still have to spend with Mom. I haven't talked about her as much as I should have in this book. No one has worked harder on my behalf, or suffered more from the setbacks, than she has. Like Grandma John before her, Mom is an inspiration. Hopefully, she'll need me for a long time to come.

I wrote a short tribute to my father after his death. Confronted by his loss, I didn't know what else to do. I guess it was meant to be a eulogy, one which was never delivered. With the hope that I managed in some small part to capture the essence of this good man, I would like to deliver it now:

How do you say Good-bye?

How do you say good-bye to the guy who lugged you all over as a child, and in my case as a teenager and an adult? Dad has always been my rock, the man who pushed me further than I ever thought possible after my bout with polio. Having lost a daughter to the disease, he and Mom would not accept the prognosis of helpless invalid for me. He may not have understood many of the paths I would take but he was always the optimist about the outcome. Things would get better; we'll "git 'em" next time. That was Dad's philosophy. With his pencil ever ready, he would calculate his expenses and profits on any available surface: the door and the inner walls of the old outhouse, the walls inside the feed shed, even the white enamel top of the kitchen table. There were never any losses in these figures, Dad didn't believe in jinxing himself. The real world could do that.

He kept the faith during the year brother Mike spent in Vietnam with the Marine Corps. As a friend put it, he was "one proud Poppy." I'm told by many that his eyes lit up when he talked about "his boys." Dad was a family man. He wore the title of "Gumpy" with pride, a name his granddaughters gave him. He loved his great grandchildren beyond measure. Actually, Dad loved children, anybody's children. If there was a kid in the room, he or she would soon have his full attention. First there was that wonderful smile with the missing front tooth on display, then the wiggling fingers, and then the talk aimed at establishing confidence. Very few kids could resist my father. Soon, most of them would be sitting in his lap sharing hugs or running around the room waving his cane, much to Dad's amusement and everybody else's concern. Thankfully, nothing was ever broken.

Farming was Dad's profession, his passion, his true calling. He left school after the eighth grade to pursue it under the strict tutelage of his father. My childhood memories of life on the farm with Dad are truly wonderful; this was before the hard times. He seemed most happy on summer days after evening chores. As the dust of the day's traffic settled into the draws between the hills, or evening mist started forming along the creek bed or the bottoms, you could usually find Dad leaning on a fence listening to the sounds of his kingdom: the soft sounds of cattle munching their supper at the feed bunks, the clanging of self-feeder lids as the hogs took turns stuffing themselves, the creaking of the pumps and the windmill bringing water to the stock, the rustling of the leaves on the giant cottonwood tree that stood guard at the top of the hill, the occasional cackle of a pheasant at the edge of the corn field. This was Dad's world and he was always reluctant to leave it to the night, even though Mom and supper were waiting. To an impatient youngster this could be very annoying, especially when promised a visit with cousins. But Dad could never be hurried. One evening I searched all over for him, finally found him sitting on a bucket in the hen house actually talking to the chickens.

That's my father, a man given to simple earthy pleasures, a man who took a "hands on" approach to animals and people alike. Everything was better with a touch, a pat, a hug, or even a kiss, and the sooner the better; only the nimble could escape Dad's embrace. He could use words and phrases never heard before or since when dealing with runaway livestock or cranky machinery, but be as gentle as the breeze with a sickly child.

His likes and dislikes are legend within the family. If a Ford backfired anywhere within a hundred miles, Dad knew about it; a Chrysler on fire in the backyard would escape his notice. He loved his John Deere machinery and Chrysler New Yorker automobiles. Ask anyone in the family about his gas mileage calculations; it's sure to bring a smile. He rarely missed *Wheel of Fortune* and *The Price is Right*, or Lawrence Welk and Guy Lombardo on television. A deck of cards was always within reach, he could play Solitaire for hours.

Cancer is such an ugly disease. Dad survived two prior bouts with surgery but this time the Lord was calling him home. His decline was swift and relentless. He enjoyed his last Christmas with the family. Everybody down to the littlest one got a special gift from "Gumpy," winnings from his run of good luck at the casino. Although food was getting hard to digest, he did eat a little steak to celebrate his 67th wedding anniversary. He was here for Mom's birthday.

The last two weeks were the worst. Dad wanted to die at home, not a hospital or a nursing home. There were many tears and whispered family conversations as we struggled to meet his wishes. Hospice was wonderful, drugs controlled his pain. Others helped out, but the burden fell heavily on Mom and my brother. Somehow, they managed to complete the mission, I've never been more proud of them. Although the process was brutal, the end was peaceful.

So, how do you say good-bye? The dictionary says the word is a contraction of the phrase "God go with you;" that's easy enough. But I can't bring myself to say farewell. He hasn't gone that far away.......just from here to our hearts.

I love you, Pop!

Dick Wieler

February 1, 2006

And so the circle of life has been completed for another I loved dearly. Knowing my past is much longer than my future, I sometimes wonder when the circle will close for me. In the meantime, I still have things to do.

21

Another Point of View

[Author's note: During the course of gathering materials for this book, Maureen Clark conducted many interviews with former colleagues and friends. Knowing that a complete list would be impossible, I tried to give her a representative sample of the many people who helped me in my quest for normality. By necessity, the list is arbitrary and in no way intended to be a slight to those not included. The book is my tribute to all of you, named and unnamed, who helped mold me into the man I am. What follows are excerpts from those interviews, as presented by Maureen. This is her chapter.]

Sometimes the best measure of a man is the mark others make for him. Although Dick Wieler attempts to summarize his life in the title, *Chasing Normality,* how would those who observed him professionally or personally summarize it? During the 22 years that he worked for the state of Missouri, he argued frequently before the Missouri Supreme Court. In describing Dick's presentations to that court, "normal" would not be a word that former Missouri Supreme Court Chief Justice Edward

Robertson would use. He wrote: "Watching Dick Wieler argue a case was a marvelous experience. He had a better grasp of the law than anyone in the room, including the seven of us wearing the black robes. He would argue without notes, make his points succinctly and knew when he'd said enough. Let me say it this way. I heard well over 1500 cases argued before the Missouri Supreme Court. Dick was the very best advocate I ever heard. No one else came close."

Another former chief justice for the Missouri Supreme Court, Ann Covington, shared an office with Dick for several months while she was in the Missouri Attorney General's Office. After joining the court, she heard many of his regular appearances before that court. Often, when asked to give speeches to young lawyers, she uses him as an example. She puts it this way, "As a professional, Dick Wieler was the ultimate. He appeared before the court always completely prepared, and always with a sense of humor that was completely appropriate. It is a rare lawyer who can quip a little bit with the court. Only a lawyer whom the court knows well and respects completely is able to get away with that. He never pushed it, but from time to time he would do that and everyone enjoyed it. He had the ability to get to the point. He was always ready to admit when the law was not on his side. He was the ultimate example of what a lawyer should be. He never misrepresented any matter of fact or law to the court.... He was unparalleled as a practitioner before the Missouri Supreme Court, as an advocate and as an appellate lawyer."

For his part, Dick takes a more humble approach to his accomplishments in court. He wrote this response to an inquiry:

"I know you've been looking for a clue to explain my success as an appellate attorney—I wish I knew. I am not a polished public speaker; I don't even like public speaking. Stage fright was a reality every time I was required to do it. Any time I could talk opposing counsel into submitting a case to the court on briefs alone, I did it. I always thought I made my points through writing. Preparation and knowledge of the subject matter are the keys. I studied the trial transcripts very carefully, looking for the facts that supported my interpretation of the law. The law of state revenue was something I knew quite well. I'm surprised that others found my court room presentations remarkable."

Even as a young attorney, Dick earned a reputation for being competent. Just four months after he started working as an assistant attorney general, Jack Danforth was voted into office as Missouri's attorney general. According to Danforth, he did not retain everyone who was in the office. He explained that his decision to keep attorneys was not based on their political affiliation, but rather on whether they were competent. Because he was told that Dick was very capable, he decided to keep him.

At that time, the salary for an assistant attorney general was quite modest. What Danforth did to attract young capable lawyers was to promise them the opportunity for experience and "more responsibility by far than what they could get in the private sector." Danforth described everyone in the office, including himself, as being very young and inexperienced. Reflecting on his tenure as Missouri's attorney general, and thinking about all the responsibility they had, he said, "Oh, my gosh, how could we have done that?" The voters certainly approved of the job done because Jack Danforth went on to serve as a U.S. senator from Missouri for 18 years.

"There was lots of idealism and camaraderie in our office," Danforth said, and Dick was "enormously popular" with his colleagues. He concluded, "What is Dick? First of all, he is very likeable, he is very able, he does very good work, and to boot, he is very inspiring!"

One of the attorneys that Jack Danforth hired while he was attorney general was Clarence Thomas. Thomas and others who worked with Dick and are his friends often describe him as being "one of the guys." In addition, they describe Dick as being the facilitator of much of the camaraderie in the office, particularly through his carpool. Typically, the carpool included four or five attorneys together in Dick's van. When one member would move away for another position, another would take his place in the carpool. The 30 minute drive from Columbia to Jefferson City and then back again provided opportunity for lively conversations on a variety of subjects. Sometimes, they would discuss sports; sometimes they would discuss work; oftentimes they discussed other topics of deep importance. The camaraderie extended beyond the carpool and embraced the other colleagues in the office. Normally, several of the attorneys would eat lunch together in the cafeteria, or in Dick's office. Their socializing continued outside of the office. There were barbecues at various homes and sometimes they went out to restaurants.

Thomas met Dick shortly after joining the office in 1974. He described watching the van pulling up to the back of the Missouri Supreme Court building so that Dick could get into the building from the loading dock. He noted that Dick never complained about it. Also, Thomas laughed as he remembered some of the homemade equipment: "He had this makeshift ramp that just about killed everyone in the office at one time or the other. It was cobbled together on the van. Everyone would get their fingers pinched in it. Everyone knew how to put the ramp down. We all knew how to seatbelt him in. Nobody was a champion, it was not a big deal; we were his friends. Everyone who was his friend helped him, took him to the men's room. He was our buddy. It wasn't a big deal. When we went to restaurants a couple of buddies would lift him and his wheelchair if there was a curb, or three or four steps. Nobody thought two seconds about it." Thomas noted, "We were all a bunch of buddies. We had to be concerned about how our friend was going to get in or out of a restaurant. Is the door wide enough? Does it open properly? That was the beginning of being aware of little things causing big problems for people who happen to be in wheelchairs." Thomas credits that awareness with his insistence that the Equal Employment Opportunity Commission office building constructed in Washington D.C. during his tenure as chairman be 100% accessible.

Thomas also related his early frustrations at being stereotyped because of his race, but then he observed "how dignified Dick was about his own situation. He didn't complain about it, didn't whine about it, he didn't hold anyone else responsible for it." He concluded: "Maybe I should emulate him. Dick was a hero in the office because he made everyone treat him like an individual. He was never the victim. He was never defensive. He was not Dick the person with a disability, he was Dick. It is so liberating, because he put you at ease. He would goof around with people and rib them. He was one of the guys. He would give people a hard time and they would give it right back....I offered him a job twice after moving to Washington because he was such a clear thinker; he turned me down both

Irven Friedhoff

"Sometimes you need a helping hand."

times....Dick is a dear friend and one of the giants in my life."

Dick explained why he had turned down the job offers: "I had to give them serious consideration because they came from Clarence. He and I share many philosophies and, based on the rapport we established in the Attorney General's Office, I knew we could work well together. However, I didn't want to move any further from Mom and Dad; I knew Dad would never drive to Washington D.C. Furthermore, I had established a system and a network of friends in Columbia that allowed me to function. I was afraid of re-establishing that system in a large and distant city. I knew Clarence would look out for me but feared it would be too great a burden. Finally, I thought I was doing important work where I was; I liked my job."

John Ashcroft was also a colleague of Dick's in the Missouri Attorney General's Office. Ashcroft served two terms

Irven Friedhoff

Fishing excursion with Butch Faddis.

Irv with the only catch of the day.

as Missouri's attorney general starting in 1976. Subsequently, he went on to serve as Missouri's governor, as a U.S. senator, and as U.S. attorney general.

During an interview he noted, "Dick has been an inspiration to me for decades." In a letter of recommendation he wrote: "I have the highest regard for Dick Wieler. He was a very good attorney. His assessment of legal matters was well-respected in the Missouri attorney general's office. He was more than willing to defend the judgments at which he had arrived—to defend them with good humor, and with the give and take found in an environment where various points of view would refine and improve the final outcome." In a second interview, Ashcroft further stated that Dick was not only very well respected as an attorney in the attorney general's office, but in Missouri government as well. He added, "He has not let disadvantages devalue or interfere with the great advantages that he has, those being a sharp mind and an irrepressible spirit."

Another attorney, Mark Siedlik, joined the Missouri Attorney General's Office in 1983. It didn't take long for the two men to learn that they had something in common: they were both from Nebraska. Siedlik was from Omaha, which is about an hour and a half from West Point, Dick's hometown. Once he discovered that Dick was unable to spend holidays with family because nobody was available to drive him, he and his family began driving Dick's van to take him home for the holidays. Once they arrived at West Point, they would trade vehicles with Dick's dad and then drive to Omaha to visit their family. After the visit, they would reverse the process. He and his wife were able to get to know Dick's parents, Richard and Marie, which he said was an extra bonus.

Four years after joining the office, Siedlik transferred from the criminal division to the governmental affairs division. He was assigned to the tax division; Dick was his supervisor and he was given the office next to Dick's. From his vantage point, he could see the constant parade of attorneys in and out of Dick's office. He commented: "I'd venture to say there wasn't a day when someone didn't stop in to ask him for help on something." Whenever he asked Dick for advice on various points of law, Siedlik was amazed that Dick could respond by suggesting that he look up a particular case, giving the name, volume number, and page number from memory. When he asked Dick how he could remember so much, Dick rattled his arms in their braces a little and responded with a grin: "It's not like I can go looking for it more than once."

Judicial review of tax cases in Missouri always occurred in the Missouri Supreme Court instead of one of the three courts of appeals. Siedlik says it was not unusual for Dick to have four cases a week before that court when it was in session. In any given term, there might be 15 tax cases that the office had before the court and Dick might argue 11 of them. Sometimes he did two a day. Siedlik commented: "The last week I was in the office, before I was appointed as an administrative judge in St. Louis, I want to say we had 11 cases to argue. I did two and he did all the rest." He remembered that if Dick did use notes while he was arguing, it was only one page. He marvels at how Dick kept them all straight.

He feels that much of Dick's courtroom style was born out of necessity. Turning pages of notes with his mouthstick would have been difficult. He also noticed that Dick spoke briefly, especially in his later years, because he didn't have the breath to be long-winded; he knew how to get to the point quickly.

Siedlik commented: "Dick Wieler was a brilliant lawyer and in particular a very good appellate lawyer. If you look back at the body of work that he did—he was there for about 20 years—his name is on about every tax case before the Missouri Supreme Court argued by the Attorney General's Office. Dick helped to develop a body of law and his name will be on those cases forever."

Siedlik is now working as an administrative law judge in Kansas City. He considers Dick a dear friend. In commenting about this book he added: "People might not be interested in tax law, but I think his abilities with the things he had to overcome make for a story that people would enjoy."

Dick had been working as an attorney for 19 years when Kevin Crane joined the office and the carpool in 1987. Fresh out of law school, Crane recalls the experience with fondness. He cherished the 30 minutes each way that he spent in the carpool, and misses the camaraderie. The time spent there gave him an opportunity to debate and to discuss a variety of topics. He described Dick as being one of the few people who has "the fine art, or rather the dying art of conversation." He noted: "When he gets an idea he will debate it to the end. He won't respect you if you won't hang with him to the end." He reflected: "With Dick's attitude and outlook, and ability to discuss hunting and fishing that he did as a kid, often times you would forget he was handicapped." Like so many others in that close-knit community, Crane has enjoyed success in the field of law. He is now a circuit court judge in Missouri.

Not only was Dick well-liked by his colleagues in the office; he was well-liked by the secretaries. Lucia Vest was Dick's longest serving secretary. She joined the Missouri Attorney General's Office in 1970, a few years after Dick started. At that time she was assigned to three other attorneys. During the next several years, she had the chance to observe Dick around the office. When he returned to the office after three years of working for the Missouri Department of Revenue, she requested a transfer to work with Dick and his team because she thought it would be pleasant to work for him. He was a friend to everyone.

"In the almost 30 years I worked in the Attorney General's Office he was the best boss. He was just a nice guy all the way around; he had a good sense of humor, he didn't hold grudges, he didn't get vicious if something went wrong. He said it, got over it, corrected it, and he went on. He appreciated what I did for him and treated me like a valuable member of his team. Working for three lawyers, sometimes it could get a wee bit hairy. Dick was understanding about the pressures that I was under."

"His sense of humor was evident the minute he wheeled in the door. He was never a sour puss, unless he was really, really sick. He sometimes came to work when he didn't feel well.... First thing in the morning, I attached his pen to a bar on his feeder (arm brace) and made sure he had a cup of water with a straw on his desk. I never minded the extra duty; it was a pleasure to do it."

It wasn't just those in the Attorney General's Office and the court who took note of his abilities. A lawyer friend, Lee Henson, is the ADA Coordinator with the University of Missouri, which means he advises the university on matters involving the Americans with Disabilities Act. He tells the story of another lawyer friend who met Dick by happenstance.

Henson was 45 years old and living in the Kansas City area with his family when he injured his spinal cord in a bicycle accident and became quadriplegic. Jim Walsh, a lawyer and a friend of Henson, visited regularly while he was in the hospital and after he returned home. Henson confided to Walsh that he was very worried about whether he would be able to continue to make a living because of his disability. He told Walsh that he had heard of only one quadriplegic lawyer in Missouri, a man named Dick Wieler.

As Henson remembers, Walsh suddenly said, "I think I've met him!" He then went on to describe the circumstances. He explained that a few years earlier he had a hearing scheduled in Jefferson City regarding a tax issue. The other side of the case was to be argued by the Missouri Attorney General's office. He didn't know who from that office would be arguing the case, and he had never met or heard of Dick Wieler. When he walked into the courtroom and saw Dick at the opposing counsel's table, sitting in his bulky power wheelchair, both arms in his metal braces, Walsh was stunned. He thought to himself, "Oh my God, that poor guy! How can I argue against him? I feel so sorry for him."

Then the hearing started. Walsh told Henson that about 10 seconds after Dick began speaking, he stopped feeling sorry for him. He said Dick was aggressive and very effective. "He was a helluva good lawyer, and I wanted to kick his butt, wheelchair or no wheelchair." Walsh then acknowledged that he lost the case.

Henson first met Dick several years after this conversation with Jim Walsh. After becoming friends, he told Dick the story. "That story had a major impact on my life and my attitude toward disability," Henson said.

Dick and Irv Friedhoff after the Order of the Coif Initiation Ceremony

Dick's abilities were acknowledged in 1998 by his alma mater, the University of Missouri School of Law. That year he was chosen to be the school's honorary initiate into the Order of the Coif. This national award is given annually to law school graduates selected from the top 10% of their class. In addition, qualifying law schools across the country can select someone annually for honorary initiation as a way to recognize their professional accomplishments. Dick's accomplishments as an appellate attorney were instrumental to his selection; he represented the state in over 200 appellate cases during his tenure, most of them before the Missouri Supreme Court.

Dick's close friend and long time neighbor, Irven Friedhoff, told me that he and Dick always ate dinner together, and spent many hours outside on their veranda. As they did so, many people wandered by to visit with them. Friedhoff said Dick made friends with everyone in the complex and was instrumental in creating a close-knit society with a friendly atmosphere at the

Gatehouse Apartments where they lived. Paradoxically, he describes Dick as a naturally private person; reaching out to people was a stretch for him. Friedhoff said he himself finds it hard to ask for help, but reflected: "You end up doing what you have to do to get through life." He observed that Dick is not afraid to ask anyone for help, and has had to do it almost every day of his life. He described Dick as "a hard worker, gutsy, with a willingness to take on things." He said: "It has always amazed me that he has been able to do as well as he has with the limitations that he has."

Where did this spirit, this spunk, come from? I pondered this question as I pursued these interviews. As Dick's mother, Marie Wieler, was approaching her 89th birthday, I had the privilege of interviewing her. Even through the phone I could see Marie's twinkle in her eye and hear her lighthearted laugh as she recalled the events of their lives. She didn't want to dwell on sad things and kept saying: "Well, you just make the most of things....We never let him give up."

At my request, she briefly recounted how they had lost their daughter at the same time that Dick got polio; how a drought had caused them to lose their crops at the same time that cattle prices fell; how they drove back and forth to visit Dick in Omaha, hoping that he would recover; how they had to sell off their machinery and then how eventually in the '80s they lost the farm that had been in their family for 100 years. She credited her late husband as always looking on the bright side. She credited their faith in God in getting them through it all. She then laughed and succinctly summed up the Wieler outlook, "There is no sense in being bitter....Those were some bad years, but we managed to have a good life."

Epilogue

Now that you've read my story, I'd like to close with a brief discussion of what it all means. As I have lived my life, many questions remain unanswered. What was the purpose of all this? What have I accomplished? These are just a few of the questions that come to mind. Everyone's life is a mystery, full of surprises and unexpected twists at every stage, and so I suppose everyone has these thoughts. In the process of writing this book, I asked my co-writer what description she would give me. Like many others, she called me a "trailblazer." By that, I assume she means someone who has set a path for others to follow. I do have a lot of firsts to my credit. I'm the first on my father's side to finish college and law school, and I did it from a wheelchair. I'm the first wheelchair user to graduate from the University of Missouri Law School, the first to work for the Missouri Attorney General's Office, and the first to appear regularly before the Missouri Supreme Court. These are accomplishments to be proud of and I am; but it would be presumptuous of me to think of myself as a shining star for others to follow.

This description focuses more on what I've done than who I am. Without the wheelchair, nothing about my life would be extraordinary. Paralysis and the wheelchair are an integral part of my story. Even so, I've done nothing more than what was hoped for me and what I expected of myself. Talent given freely by God should not be squandered regardless of the obstacles.

At the same time, I am reminded of the many hands that made this possible. Without their help, my trail would have led nowhere. It humbles me greatly to be told that I have been an inspiration to others. This book is my opportunity to say "thank you" to all those who helped me become the man I am.

Utilizing the Western theme, I describe myself as a "drag rider" instead of a "trailblazer." For those of you unfamiliar with the term, the drag rider was the cowboy responsible for pushing the herd onward during the cattle drives from Texas and Oklahoma to the railheads in Kansas and Missouri. Riding drag behind the herd was dusty, smelly work. Keeping the herd moving and preventing stragglers from bolting was hard and lonely work and the view was less than inspiring. Like the drag rider, I have labored often in solitude and in less than pristine conditions. At times, the view from a wheelchair can be dreary. It's not uncommon for people to keep a safe distance from me, carefully staying upwind. I've learned to accept that, it's perfectly understandable.

My disability is mine to carry, and mine alone. By accepting my limitations, I am free to pursue the things I can. Dwelling on the way I wish things were, or were not, only limits that freedom. My old baseball coach used to put it this way: "Boys, 'if' never 'did.'" Wishful thinking is a diversion, a retreat from reality. We all live in the real world; it must be dealt with as such.

I may be different but I am still a working member of the community. Like the drag rider, I use the same chuck wagon and share the same campfire with the rest of the group. And so it is with the human society of which I am a part. We all share one fundamental trait: life. And we also share a common desire: the desire for liberty and the pursuit of happiness.

I was very reluctant to write about my life because of fear that this commonality would be overlooked in the telling of my struggle. Pity is the last emotion I wanted to evoke. It may make the giver feel better but, unaccompanied by constructive activity, it does nothing for the recipient. It took a great deal of urging by family and friends, and a dedicated co-writer, to accomplish this. I hope you found it informative, and entertaining. At heart, I am a simple farmer's son; the practice of law was a fallback position. It was an impossible dream forged by a teenage boy who was battered almost beyond recognition by a cruel disease. The dream came true by the grace of God, hard work and sacrifice, and the help of many.

I leave you with two of the many quotations that hold great meaning for me:

> Keep on the sunny side, always on the sunny side
> Keep on the sunny side of life.
> It will help us every day. It will brighten all our way.
> If we keep on the sunny side of life

(From the song "Keep on the Sunny Side" lyrics by Ada Blenkhorn & J. Howard Entwisle ©1899)

"To those whom much is given, much is expected."

(The Gospel of St. Luke, 12:48)

Peace.

Acknowledgments

To see one's story in print is a strange but exhilarating feeling. It never appealed to me to write a memoir in spite of frequent requests from family and friends. I didn't think it would be that interesting. If not for the tireless efforts of Maureen Clark, this book would not have become a reality. Among other things, she brought discipline and structure to the project, thereby allowing me the freedom to express my thoughts. It rapidly became a quest for an honest but uplifting story; I hope you are pleased with our collaborative effort.

It was a great disappointment when the manuscript was rejected by several publishers. The decision to make it a family project and enter the world of self-publishing was made with the help of Kevin Buchanan, a former colleague and friend of long-standing. Kevin untied the Gordian knot that entangled us and showed us the way to organize our own publishing company.

It is with great joy that I bring my family into this project. We have endured the bad times and enjoyed the good times together. It is fitting that we take this last great adventure together.

Dick Wieler

About us

RMKM6 Publishing LLC is a family business formed for the purpose of publishing, promoting and selling this book. We have grown up watching Dick cope with his condition in an admirable manner and we wanted to give the world the chance to share our feelings of pride in his many accomplishments.

If you liked this book, please tell all your friends and neighbors how to purchase additional copies at

www.chasingnormality.com
or
www.RichardWieler.com

The price per book is $18.95 plus $5 shipping & handling Nebraska residents must add 5.5% sales tax.

Books can also be purchased directly by sending cash or money order to the following address:

RKMK6 Publishing LLC
1174 I Road
West Point, Nebraska 6878

To encourage bulk sales,
we offer a discount for any purchase of 10 books or more.
Thank you very much for your support!